United States of America

the land and its people

John Bear

Macdonald Educational

Contents

Settling the land

Native and other Americans

The only native Americans are the Red Indians and the Hawaiians. No one else can trace his American ancestry back further than 1607, the founding of the first permanent colony at Jamestown, Virginia.

America grew slowly in its early years, as settlers arrived from Western Europe and slaves were brought from Africa. By the time of the War of Independence (1776), there were fewer than four million Americans, mostly living along the Atlantic seaboard.

But when the United States was born, it began to grow rapidly. The land was rich and huge, especially after President Jefferson purchased over two million square kilometres (800,000 square miles)—an area nine times as large as Great Britain—from France, in 1803.

Spurred by the discovery of gold in California (1849), encouraged by the Homestead Act (1863) which gave anyone 160 acres of land, free, if they would live on it for five years, millions of Europeans streamed to "the new world" to join the native-born Americans on the great road west.

The melting pot

Many immigrants kept a spot in their hearts for what they called "the old country" and even today, generations removed from the land of their forefathers, millions of Americans identify themselves as "Irish-Americans", "Polish-Americans" "Chinese-Americans" and so forth. Descendants of slaves and other blacks identify as "Afro-Americans".

This influence may be seen in the many foreign, or "ethnic" neighbourhoods that can be found in most cities, often with local names like "Chinatown" or "Little Italy".

Immigration reached its peak with 1,285,000 arrivals in the year 1907. In recent years, only 300,000 persons a year have been allowed to immigrate. An interesting aspect of this "melting pot" of nations is that the United States now has more Jews than Israel, more Irish-Americans than there are people in Ireland, and literally tens of millions of "German-Americans (25 million), British-Americans (31 million) and Afro-Americans (23 million).

▲ Spanish explorer Hernando De Soto (1500?-1542) became wealthy in the Spanish conquest of Peru. Appointed governor of Florida, he headed west searching for gold, and by accident became the first European to see the Mississippi River.

▶ William Penn (1644-1718), having been imprisoned in England for his Quaker beliefs, later was given a royal grant of land as a haven for Quakers in the New World. In Penn's Woods, or Pennsylvania, Penn signed the first of many treaties with the Indians—treaties so fair, his colony was never attacked.

▼ The U.S. Government bought nearly two million acres of Oklahoma land from the Indians for use by white settlers. People lined up on the borders by the thousands, and when a gun was fired on the morning of 22 April 1889, they began a mad dash across the land to stake their claims.

▲ Pioneers headed west in covered wagons, across the great plains and prairies of the Midwest, and the vast deserts and tall mountains of the far west. Paid guides led "trains" of up to several hundred wagons on this perilous journey. The ruts worn by wagons can still be seen in many places.

▶ More than 27 million people emigrated to the United States in the half century between 1880 and 1930. A great many of them passed through English ports, such as these Poles and Czechs boarding their ship enroute for New York. Many would later go on to Chicago and the Midwest.

▼ Many Americans also retain some of the life-style of their country of origin or ancestry. Nearly three fourths of America's half-million Chinese-Americans live in the states of California, Hawaii and New York, often in "Chinatown" sections like this. Every state has some Chinese population.

Where the immigrants came from, 1830-1910

GREAT BRITAIN 5,000,000

GERMANY 4,000,000

AUSTRIA/HUNGARY 3,200,000

RUSSIA 2,700,000

IRELAND 2,000,000

CANADA 1,200,000

SWEDEN 1,000,000

▲ Seven countries supplied the majority of emigrants with nearly half coming just from Great Britain and Germany.

A country of many extremes

Different, and proud of it

There are 50 states which have joined together to form the United States. But each state is very different from all the others, and proud of it. Each state has its own laws (there are some national laws as well), customs, schools, taxes, police, traffic regulations, and so forth. Even the words people use and the accents they speak them in can be quite different state to state.

The United States is huge. From New York in the east to Hawaii in the west is as far as from London to Peking. You can travel nearly one and a half thousand kilometres and never leave the state of California.

Nature's extremes

On a day when there is a raging blizzard in North Dakota and temperatures of 20 below zero (F.) in Maine, people can be relaxing on the warm beaches of Florida.

It is hard to describe any one region of the U.S. because they can differ so much, even within a short distance. From swelteringly hot Death Valley, California, the lowest point in the U.S. (282 feet below sea level) to snow-capped Mount Whitney, the highest point outside of Alaska, is less than 100 miles.

The illustrations on these pages show some typical scenes from different regions. But many other quite different scenes can be found in all these areas. There are rugged mountains in New England, farms in New York state, beaches in Alaska, deserts in Oregon, and great cities in the Midwest.

The American people

The 50 states vary widely in size and population. Texas has 250 times as much land as Rhode Island. New Jersey has nearly 400 people per square kilometre (.38 square miles); Alaska has less than one person per 2.5 square kilometres!

Each state has an elected governor and state legislature, to make the state's laws, with courts to enforce them. Every state has its own flag, song, animal, bird and motto. There is at least one state university in each state, whose athletic teams are avidly supported. But, partly because Americans move house so often, there is often no strong feeling of loyalty to one's state.

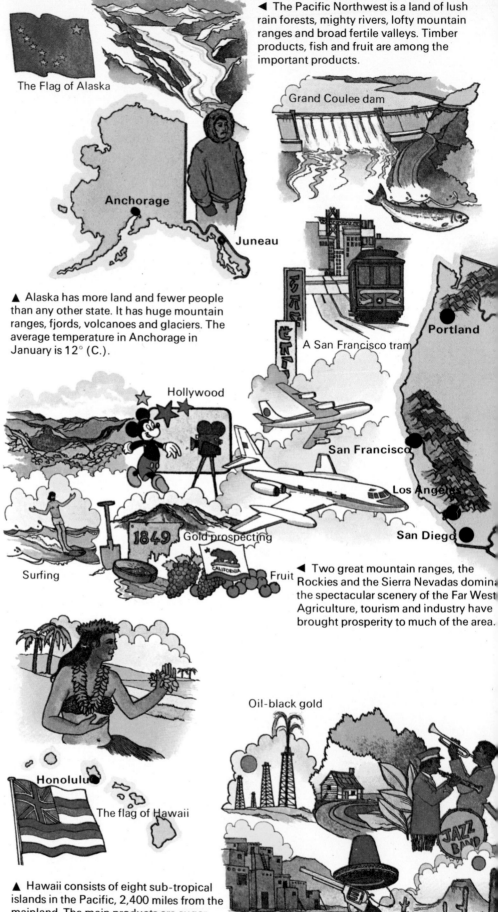

The Flag of Alaska

◀ The Pacific Northwest is a land of lush rain forests, mighty rivers, lofty mountain ranges and broad fertile valleys. Timber products, fish and fruit are among the important products.

Grand Coulee dam

Anchorage

Juneau

▲ Alaska has more land and fewer people than any other state. It has huge mountain ranges, fjords, volcanoes and glaciers. The average temperature in Anchorage in January is 12° (C.).

A San Francisco tram

Portland

Hollywood

San Francisco

Los Angeles

San Diego

Surfing

1849   Gold prospecting

Fruit

◀ Two great mountain ranges, the Rockies and the Sierra Nevadas dominate the spectacular scenery of the Far West. Agriculture, tourism and industry have brought prosperity to much of the area.

Honolulu

The flag of Hawaii

▲ Hawaii consists of eight sub-tropical islands in the Pacific, 2,400 miles from the mainland. The main products are sugar and pineapples. Average January temperature in Honolulu is 73° (F.).

Oil-black gold

▽ A desert landscape

▼ Huge farms cover the landscape of the American Midwest. Corn, wheat, soybeans and sorghum grain are the biggest crops. There are also mighty industrial centres such as Chicago, Detroit and St. Louis.

Sioux Indians

The Corn Belt

The motor industry

▼ The six New England states bear many similarities to the "old" England from which many of its original settlers came: the style of the houses, the names of towns, even the accents of the people.

Forests of Maine

The Mayflower

Niagara falls

Washington—the Capitol

Minneapolis

Milwaukee

Detroit

Chicago

Indianapolis

St. Louis

Boston

New York

Washington

Memphis

Dallas

Houston

San Antonio

New Orleans

▲ The East Coast is so crowded and industrialised, one can drive the 440 miles from Boston to Washington without ever leaving a populated area. Some people even call this the "City of Bos-Wash".

Mississippi river-boat

The Flag of Florida

The New York skyline

Miami

Beaches

NASA

The Everglades

Cotton

◄ The states of the Deep South once seceded to form a separate country; in many ways they are still a world apart. The pace of life is slower, the climate warmer, and the accents hard for a "Yankee" to understand.

◄ The Florida Everglades preserve much of the primeval swampland that once covered much of the southeast. But modern Florida thrives on Citrus farming, tourism and heavy industry.

The American influence

America in world politics

In his famous Farewell Address in 1796, George Washington warned America against permanent "foreign entanglements". But for nearly two centuries, the U.S. *has* been entangled in the affairs of the world—political, military, scientific, and cultural.

For much of the nineteenth century, the U.S. kept out of the world arena and concentrated on internal matters. President Monroe had declared (in 1823) that the U.S. would not look favourably on any attempts by Europe to colonize the Americas.

Spanish rule (or misrule) in Cuba led to war with Spain (1898-1900) and America was firmly enmeshed in world politics. For the next sixty years, America often seemed to regard itself as the protector of the rest of the world, but the long Vietnam war (1963-73) probably ended all thoughts of bringing the "American way of life" to other nations.

As the wealthiest country in the world the American economy seemed to be, for many years, the foundation of the financial world. More than £60 thousand million in foreign aid of all kinds was spent since 1945 to help many countries recover from the war and arm themselves for possible future wars. But the rapid economic growth of countries such as Japan and West Germany has reduced the importance and influence of the American dollar in recent years.

Science and technology

American scientific and technical achievements have had dramatic influences on world progress. From the cotton gin (the first machine with interchangeable parts), to the idea of the assembly line, to the lunar landing module, the products of American inventiveness and technology have touched the lives of most of the world's peoples.

American cultural influence is perhaps not as strong. It has been argued that America has not yet produced any truly great artists, writers or musicians—but then it is a very young nation, by world standards.

▲ America "won" the space race when astronauts Neil Armstrong and "Buzz" Aldrin set foot on the lunar surface in July 1969.

◄ Wall Street, in New York, is the financial centre of America and its influence is worldwide. Seen here are people waiting for news of the stock market "crash" in 1929.

▼ 30 years after the war, U.S. troops still operate Checkpoint Charlie between E. and W. Berlin.

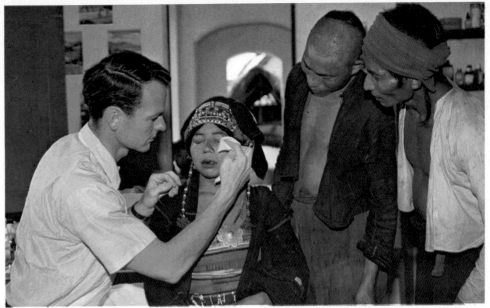

◀ The atomic bombs dropped in 1945 on the Japanese cities of Hiroshima and Nagasaki (shown here) were the only atomic weapons used in war. President Truman, who ordered the bombings, argued that by ending the war they saved more lives than they took.

▲ As the wealthiest country in the world, America feels responsible for the poorer nations. CARE—the Cooperative for American Relief Everywhere—distributes food and medical supplies paid for by individual donations from American citizens.

Some American gifts to the world

▲ People everywhere have learned about America through the thousands of films made in the studios of Hollywood.

▲ Until the energy crisis of 1974, the huge petrol-guzzling American car was a shiny symbol of the nation's wealth.

▲ Jazz music began in New Orleans, and came up the Mississippi River with Louis Armstrong to St. Louis and the world.

▲ Anywhere in the world, this would be recognized as the "standard" American meal: a burger and a bottle of Coke.

Home life

▼ The typical middle-class American home is a detached house of indeterminate style, small lawn front and rear, shiny car in the driveway, and a big mortgage on it all.

The American lifestyle

The typical American family is simply the two parents, and two or three children, living in a detached house, with two cars in the garage, a colour television (and probably a black and white as well), two or three telephones, and a houseful of gadgets.

In large cities, there are blocks up to 100 storeys high, containing flats, shops, offices, car parks, sometimes even schools. One need never go outside at all.

Children are almost never sent away to school, but remain at home until high school graduation (age 17 or 18), when a majority go on to college or university.

Grandparents may live nearby, but rarely live in the same home with their children and grandchildren. Many older people live in "retirement communities"—housing estates or even entire towns or villages restricted to persons over 50 or 55. No children are permitted.

An average family budget

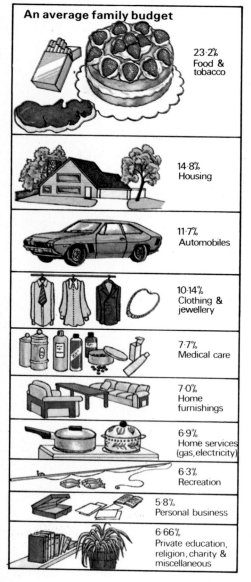

23.2%
Food & tobacco

14.8%
Housing

11.7%
Automobiles

10.14%
Clothing & jewellery

7.7%
Medical care

7.0%
Home furnishings

6.9%
Home services (gas, electricity)

6.3%
Recreation

5.8%
Personal business

6.66%
Private education, religion, charity & miscellaneous

The automated kitchen

◄ A high percentage of a family's budget goes for medical care, since there is no national health care programme, except for persons over 65. Far more is spent on tobacco than on education.

▲ Americans love gadgets about the house. Some newer ones are trash mashers, that squeeze garbage into a small cube and pack it in neat bags, and central vacuum systems with outlets in each room in the house.

Families on the move

The average American family moves once every six or seven years, and as a result, homes often don't appear to be lived in. A recent trend is huge furniture rental centres, where you can hire everything from tableware to beds. Then, when you move, you can turn your goods in, and then hire the identical items at the other end, thus saving the cost of moving.

Besides a living room, for more formal occasions, many homes have a family room —a large room where the whole family can gather for games, crafts, music, or viewing television. It is not uncommon for everyone to eat the evening meal in front of the television (in fact, packaged frozen meals are called T.V. dinners), but many Americans tend to look down their noses at this practice.

Children normally are home from school by 3:30, and most fathers get home from work between 5:30 and 6. Though bedtimes are rather early, there is time available in evenings for activities involving the entire family. In nice weather, this might include a backyard barbecue, followed by everyone piling in the car and going off to a neighbourhood drive-in movie, viewing the film from the car.

Gadgets for every need

American homes are often filled with a wide variety of gadgets of all kinds: intercom systems, garbage mashers, 20 cubic foot refrigerator-freezers with ice water, ice cube and crushed ice dispensers, heated vibrating waterbeds, electric drapery openers, saunas, electric knives, grinders, shredders, slicers and tin openers; even closed circuit television for keeping an eye on the front door, the nursery, and other rooms.

A typical daily timetable

▲ Many Americans are up by 7:00 to allow time for a big breakfast. The typical working day is 9:00 to 5:00, with lunch from noon to 1:00. Many people go to bed following the end of the 11 p.m. news on television, but millions stay up beyond this watching the late shows.

◄ Fewer and fewer American families are as large as this one, nowadays. Threatened with overcrowding everywhere from the shops to the National Parks, Americans have been having smaller families in recent years. In fact, Zero Population Growth—an average of just over two children per family—was achieved in the early 1970s, much to the surprise of the forecasters at the Census Bureau.

Leisure and pleasure

At the flick of a switch

To begin with, America has more than 7,000 commercial radio and television stations. You can't receive all of them from any one place, but in many areas there is a choice of 50 radio stations and perhaps ten television channels, some of which are on 24 hours a day. Needless to say, Americans do a great deal of watching and listening.

When the set is finally turned off, many families turn to outdoor recreation. In the winter, this may mean heading off in their snowmobile (a small vehicle with tank treads in the rear and skis in the front). Hundreds of thousands are now in use, to the distress of those who like their woods quiet. In summer, there is boating or, for ever increasing numbers, private flying.

Competition and togetherness

Americans often do things together as family units, whether they choose ten-pin bowling, square-dancing, or playing table games. Because Americans tend to be rather competitive, these activities are often organized into leagues, with prizes for the winners.

In recent years, companies and factories have introduced a 4-day working week (four 9 or 10 hour days) which means even more uninterrupted leisure time for the family. Now many families are buying second homes in recreational areas, often seashore or mountains, a few hours from their main home.

There is nothing in America quite like the European café or English pub, as a neighbourhood social gathering place. However, many Americans regard their bowling evenings, or scrabble or cards played at clubs, as mostly social occasions.

Some popular pastimes

▲ Bridge, canasta, poker, scrabble, Monopoly, and Mah Jongg are among the most popular games.

▲ Drive-in movies are for families without baby sitters and for teen-agers in love.

▲ Ten-pin bowling is among America's most popular sports, with everyone from 5-year-olds to pensioners competing in weekly leagues.

▲ Many people get their first car at age 16, and often "soup it up" or customize it.

American television

Many cities have 20 or more channels, some operating 24 hours a day. Here are one city's programmes for a typical Sunday afternoon.

4 p.m.
(4) News
(5) Other people, other places (travel)
(6) Sesame Street (child)
(7) Auto racing
(8) Meet the Press (news conference)
(12) Sports Magazine
(20) Orizzonti Christiani (Spanish)
(40) Wings to Adventure
(44) Film (Alan Ladd)
(46) Challenging Sea (adventure)

4.30 p.m.
(4) Wildlife Theater
(5) Perry Mason
(8) World of Survival
(12) Sports Spectacular
(40) Survival
(46) You can communicate
    (educational)

5.00 p.m.
(2) News in Chinese
(6) Misterogers Neighborhood (child)
(8) Wally's Workshop (craft)
(9) Washington Connection
    (discussion)
(2) Family Drama
(36) Film (western)
(46) Basketball

5.30 p.m.
(3) Wild Kingdom (animal documen-
    tary)
(4) News
(5) The Energy Crisis
(6) Electric Company (child
    educational)
(7) Issues and Answers (political
    analysis)
(8) News
(9) Yoga
(10) News
(13) High Chaparral (western series)
(40) Lassie

6.00 p.m.
(2) Movie: Anzio
(3) Men of the Sea
(4) News
(5) 60 Minutes (analysis)
(6) Carascolendas (Spanish language)
(7) Ozzie's Girls (comedy)
(8) Land of the Giants
(9) French Chef (cookery)
(11) Film: adventure
(12) Eye on Sports
(20) News from Japan
(40) Outdoor Adventure
(44) Gomer Pyle (comedy)

*The numbers in brackets refer to
different channels.*

▲ More than 1,700 daily newspapers have a total circulation over 60 million. Over 50 magazines have a million circulation, with *Reader's Digest* and *TV Guide* the top sellers.

▼ For many Americans, the idea of "getting away from it all" means towing a folding trailer-tent to the side of a lake, and fishing, boating, swimming and unwinding.

Sports and sportsmen

▲ There are eleven players in a football team. The quarterback is in charge, and must decide, for each play, whether to run with the ball, pass it to an end, or hand it to a halfback or fullback, who may then run or pass. Each manouevre is carefully planned in a huddle, held before each play. Uniforms are designed to prevent injuries in this bruising sport.

▶ The Astrodome, in Houston, Texas, is a fully enclosed air-conditioned stadium seating 50,000 people. It is used for Houston Astros baseball games and for many other sports. The playing area is covered with plastic grass called "Astroturf". The electronic scoreboard can also be used, as here, for animated cartoons.

Baseball, the national pastime

Americans like nearly all sports, except the world's most popular one, football.

Baseball, said to be invented by a retired army general in the 1870s, is called the "national pastime". Boys (and sometimes girls) can join the little leagues when they are 8. There are dozens of professional leagues, including two major leagues of 12 teams each, whose star players often earn more than £40,000 a year.

The object of baseball is to strike the ball and run to first base, then second base, third base, and "home"—which scores one run.

If a struck ball is caught, or thrown to a base before a player gets there, he is out. Three outs make an innings and nine innings make a game. There are nine players a side, but substitutions can be made from 16 other players "on the bench".

Sporting honours

In American football, one team has four tries to advance the ball ten yards. If they succeed, they keep the ball; if they fail, the other team gets it. The ball can be run or passed (thrown) down the field.

Several hundred college football games are played every Saturday afternoon. A popular game may attract 80,000 or more fans.

Most high schools and colleges have teams in basketball (another American invention), swimming, tennis, track and field (athletics), and various minor sports. Inter-school games often attract great interest.

When an athlete does well in sport, he or she is "awarded the letter"—(the school's initial) worn proudly on a sweater or jacket.

Ten-pin bowling is said to be the most popular participant sport, while auto racing attracts the largest total attendance.

▲ Basketball was invented in 1891 by James Naismith, a teacher looking for a good indoor team game. Nearly every high school and college has a team, and there are several professional leagues. Girls' basketball is popular in Midwestern states.

Famous sporting personalities

▲ Muhammed Ali is probably the most popular, controversial, and highest-paid heavyweight boxing champion America has produced.

▲ Mark Spitz earned seven gold medals for swimming at the 1972 Olympic Games; then earned a fortune by endorsing various products.

▲ Arnold Palmer is an extremely popular and successful golfer. A crowd, called "Arnie's Army" follows him around the golf course.

▲ Billie Jean King is one of America's outstanding athletes, having won many national and international tennis championships.

Education for a changing society

Free state schools

Every child in America must go to school from age 6 to 16, but most stay in school until high school graduation at 17 or 18, and nearly half go on to college.

Schools are free, run by local or state governments. There are very few private schools in America. The Founding Fathers decreed a "separation of church and state" so there is very little religious teaching or influence in public schools.

Diplomas and graduation

There are no national standards or examinations. Each school or school system sets its own requirements for graduation, and a high school diploma is often enough to get into college. Many jobs require a high school diploma as well.

There are many ultra-modern schools using computer-assisted courses, and team teaching (2 or 3 teachers per class). But one still finds one-room country schools, with pupils of all ages in the same classroom. Many larger schools have special classes for gifted and for handicapped pupils.

In most areas, pupils who live far from school have a free school bus service.

After elementary school and high school, nearly half the high school graduates go on to one of the more than 2,000 colleges or universities. Some, such as the University of Minnesota or the University of Wisconsin, have more than 60,000 students on campus.

The American school system

Typically, children will go to nursery school for one year, kindergarten for one year, elementary school for six years, three years each in junior and senior high school, and then four years at university. Would-be doctors or lawyers then spend three or four more years at graduate school.

Nursery school   3–4

Kindergarten   5–6

High school   15–18

Junior high school   12–15

Elementary school   6–12

Trade school   18+

University   18+

Postgraduate training   22+

▶ In most rural and suburban areas, children are brought to school in free big yellow buses. One method of giving everyone an equal education has been to use these buses in cities to bring some children from poorer neighbourhoods to schools in wealthier areas, and vice versa. This "bussing" has become a very emotional political issue.

◀ State schools traditionally get their operating money from local property taxes, so that schools in wealthy neighbourhoods tend to be larger, fancier and newer than those in poor areas. But the majority of schools, like this high school in New York are modern, and recent court decisions are likely to help correct the inequalities.

▼ Many children bring their lunch from home in small metal lunchboxes, with room for a sandwich, fresh fruit, a thermos jug of milk, and a sweet. They often join other children who buy their lunch from school cafeterias like this one, eating either inside or out as the weather permits.

▲ Founded in 1857, the University of Chicago achieved prominence in the 1930s under the guidance of Robert M. Hutchins, as a pioneer in innovative liberal arts programmes. Its buildings were modelled after Oxford.

◀ Many elementary and most high schools have special rooms for arts and crafts, such as this pottery class. Even college-bound students often take wood or metal shop, auto repair, jewellery, and so forth.

21

Holidays
see America first!

Driving all day

American children get a fortnight's holiday at Christmas and possibly a week around Easter, and then one long, long holiday—nearly three months—in summer. But many workers only get a two or three week holiday, so sometimes mother and the children go off to the country for several months, with father joining them at weekends.

Some parents send their children to summer camps, usually in pleasant rural areas far from the big cities, where they learn sports and craft skills, normally for terms of four, six or eight weeks.

But the most common kind of holiday is simply to get in the car and go somewhere. Many families pull caravans or drive small "pick up" trucks with portable camping units in the back. But most just drive all day and then stop, wherever they happen to be, at one of the thousands of motels that dot the American landscape. It is always possible to find a clean, comfortable bed for the night.

See America first

Often (but not always) the final destination is chosen in advance. Some people prefer natural attractions, such as one of the 39 national parks, many of which have camping facilities. Yellowstone Park, which covers an area half the size of Wales, still can get so crowded, you have to book your summer campsite months in advance.

Besides the national parks, there are hundreds of national monuments, battlefields, seashores, memorials, and scenic trails, as well as some superb state parks.

Other families prefer man-made attractions. The most popular are Disneyland (California) and Disney World (Florida) which attract more than 20 million visitors a year.

Around ten million Americans have passports for foreign travel. Millions more take their holidays in the only foreign countries Americans can drive to, Canada and Mexico. But the great majority go along with the slogan, "See America First".

Some holiday areas of America

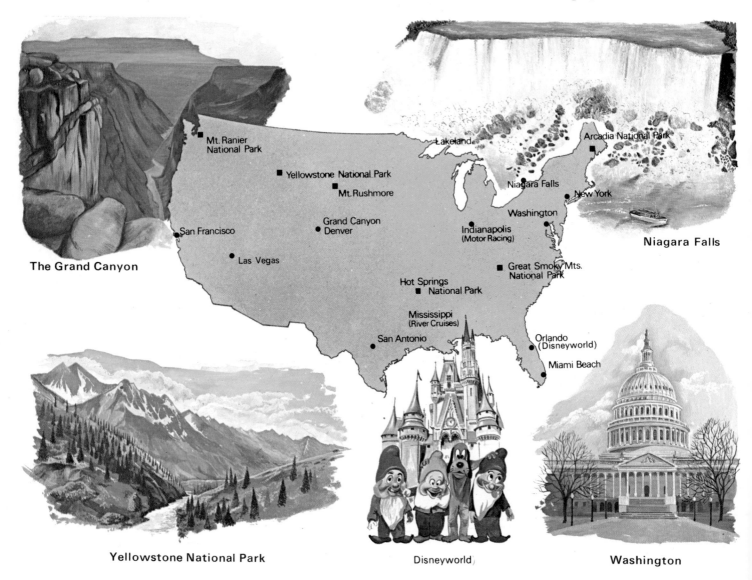

The Grand Canyon

Niagara Falls

Yellowstone National Park

Disneyworld

Washington

▲ Disneyland, near Los Angeles, was the nation's first super amusement park. Most customers are adults, but children love it too.

◄ Yellowstone, the world's first national park, was created in 1872, and covers more than a million square kilometres.

► Gambling is legal in the state of Nevada, and the city of Las Vegas has risen in the desert to become America's gambling centre.

▼ The 60-foot-high heads of Presidents Washington, Jefferson, T. Roosevelt and Lincoln were carved into South Dakota's Mt. Rushmore.

Shopping on a grand scale

The shopping trip

Let's follow a typical family on a shopping trip. The entire family gets in the car and drives to a nearby shopping centre, which may have as many as 300 shops, including two or three huge department stores. Often, the malls are enclosed, and heated or air conditioned, depending on the season.

They park in a multi-level free carpark, and head off in different directions. Mother and baby go to the supermarket, where baby is left in a supervised "Kiddie Korral" with toys and games, while mother shops.

She wheels a huge cart around, buying groceries for the week, and often clothing, hardware, plants and books as well. After paying at the checkout stand, she is given a number. Later she will drive by and her groceries, packed in big paper bags, will be put into her car by a young man.

Meanwhile, father has bought timber and new tools, sister has been attending a free class in sewing at the centre's education hall, and brother has been seeing a cartoon show at one of the four cinemas.

The whole family meets for lunch at the big cafeteria, then drives by to collect the groceries, and heads for home.

Enormous supermarkets

Of course there are still many small stores in America. The small-town general store, selling everything from sausages to shotguns, and serving as a social centre for the community as well, still survives. But Americans demand a huge choice of goods. A supermarket may stock 20,000 different items—ten times as many as a European counterpart—and the smaller shops just can't compete.

Many shops are open seven days a week until 9 or 10 in the evening, and nearly every larger town has big supermarkets and other shops that stay open 24 hours a day.

Open air markets, early closing days, and personal service are three things that have nearly disappeared from the American scene.

▲ Indoor shopping centres, such as this one in San Jose, California, may have 300 stores, cinemas, offices, amusement centres.

▲ American paper money is all the same size and colour, which is confusing. The "silver" coins are mostly copper and nickel.

The American "fast food" scene

24

▲ Ice cream shops often feature as many as fifty different flavours, including such things as peanut butter, licorice, bubble gum, and blueberry cheesecake ice cream.

▲ Many stores take a most individual approach to their signs. This pawn shop in Texas is a rather extreme example, but shops like this can be found in most larger cities.

▼ Giant supermarkets can be found throughout America. They carry as many as 20,000 items, and frequently are open seven days a week, from early morning until late at night.

Eating the American way

Native American food

Many Americans would probably be surprised to learn that pizza, chow mein, tacos and curry are not native American food. America has taken food from all over the world and adopted it as its own.

It is easier to point to an American *style* of eating than to any peculiarly American foods. Meals are informal, often cooked outdoors (barbecues). Convenience foods, such as frozen 3-course dinners that simply need to be heated, are increasingly common.

There are many regional specialties, typically found in just one part of the country: clam chowder in New England, shoo-fly pie in Pennsylvania, gumbo creole in Louisiana, barbecued bones in the Southwest, fried hominy grits in the South.

Americans eat out a great deal—breakfast, lunch, dinner, or late night snacks. Many restaurants are open 24 hours a day, and there are tens of thousands of "fast food" places, specializing in low-cost good quality hamburgers, hot dogs, fried chicken, pancakes, pizza, and other favourites.

Typical meals for a day

Breakfast:
Fresh orange juice, a stack of pancakes with bacon or egg, and coffee.

Lunch:
Hot dog on a bun, with coleslaw and baked beans, and a thick milkshake.

Dinner:
A rare grilled steak, a big baked potato with sour cream and chives, a green vegetable, salad, ice cream and coffee.

The many types of American food

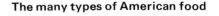

▲ Chinese restaurants can be found in all towns and cities, and sometimes even Chinese people eat in them!

▲ Spaghetti is one of America's most popular foods, among children and adults of all national backgrounds.

▲ Levy's Jewish Rye Bread became popular through the use of posters like this, featuring Irish, Blacks, Indians, etc.

▲ Take out and home-delivered pizzas are a regular meal for many Americans. A family pizza may measure 75 mm. across.

▲ Fast food stand-up restaurants offer something for everyone. A knish is a Jewish dish— potato or meat wrapped in dough and fried.

◄ Most neighbourhoods offer a wide range of places to eat, ranging from elegant continental style restaurants like this to informal "fast food" family-style hamburger joints.

▼ "Steak cafeterias" like this are popular in many cities, with the food cooked right in the window to tempt passers-by. A big steak, baked potato, green salad, garlic bread and coffee might cost well under £1.00.

Make yourself an American meal

MIDWESTERN-STYLE VEGETABLE SOUP

In a big pot, place the following (fresh if possible; frozen or tinned will do):
1 lb. carrots (sliced)
2 medium potatoes (peeled, diced)
6 medium tomatoes (quartered)
1 cup corn kernels
1 cup peas
1 pound or more of soup bones (most butchers sell or give these away)
½ to 1 cup of any vegetables you like, including beets (sliced), cabbage shredded), onions (quartered), string beans, marrow beans, okra, and so forth. Add 1 tsp. salt, ½ tsp. pepper, and if you have it, 1 dessert spoon each of basil and oregano Add 6 to 8 pints of water, bring to a boil cover, and simmer on very low heat for at least four hours. Serve with bread, butter and cheese.

THE GREAT AMERICAN HAMBURGER

For the perfect American hamburger, you must have very lean beef; try asking the butcher to grind some just for you. One pound makes three big hamburgers. Grill the patties for about 5 minutes on each side. Sprinkle salt generously on side two just before grilling. Use a big soft roll or thickly-sliced white bread, lightly toasted. Build the hamburger as follows:
Bottom half of roll thickly coated with mayonnaise (not salad cream)
Lettuce leaves
Hamburger patty
Thickly-sliced tomato
Thinly-sliced onion (raw)
Thinly-sliced pickles (sour)
Top half of roll with mustard.
Do not cut it in half. Pick it up, eat it and let the juices run down your arm!

THE CLASSIC BANANA SPLIT

The classic banana split, as made at soda fountains all over America, requires:
3 flavours of ice cream (usually chocolate, vanilla and strawberry)
3 kinds of topping (usually chocolate sauce, butterscotch sauce, and strawberry jam or syrup)
Whipped cream, chopped almonds or walnuts and a big red cherry
Slice the banana in half the long way and put one half on each side of a big (preferably oval) bowl. Place a big scoop of each ice cream in a row between the split banana. Generously pour strawberry sauce on the chocolate, butterscotch on the vanilla and chocolate on the strawberry. Cover with whipped cream, sprinkle on chopped nuts, and top with the big red cherry.

The search for American arts

Writers and painters

America's artists have never achieved the fame of her writers. From Herman Melville and Walt Whitman to the "big three" of recent years, Hemingway, Faulkner and Steinbeck, American writers have had a major impact on the world's literary scene.

The best-known American artists represent many diverse styles: the pop art of Andy Warhol; Jackson Pollock's abstractionism; the realism of three generations of the Wyeth family; and the primitives of Grandma Moses who took up painting at 78 and did some of her best work past age 100.

Hollywood used to be the centre of the world's film industry, and Broadway, in New York, was a focus of stage plays. But the importance of both has declined in recent years. Many films are still made in Hollywood, but even more are made in New York, and "on location" all over the country.

Amateurs and professionals

There are many fewer big Broadway plays nowadays, but every town and village has its little theatre group, and live drama is very much alive in America.

American music has always expressed the moods of the people, from the stirring "Yankee Doodle" of the War of Independence to the ballads and patriotic songs of both sides in the Civil War to the haunting "We Shall Overcome", the song of the modern Civil Rights movement.

Jazz is said to be America's only original music form, but composers from Stephen Foster to Leonard Bernstein have contributed much to the world's music.

Americans are inclined to be very interested in acquiring "culture". Millions of people enrol each year in night school and private courses in writing, painting, dance, film making, or various crafts. Many children start music lessons at age 6 or 7, and may learn two or three instruments before they are 16. There are no fewer than 108 symphony orchestras and 64 opera companies in America.

▲ The Guggenheim Museum in New York was the last great work of architect Frank Lloyd Wright. One walks up and down the spiral pathways viewing the works of art.

▼ Grant Wood has been called America's "Painter of the Soil". His famous *American Gothic*, painted in 1930, depicts a typical hardworking Midwestern farmer and his wife.

▼ John Steinbeck (1902-68) is best known for his realistic novels of life among America's poor: like *Of Mice and Men*, *The Grapes of Wrath*.

▲ Walt Whitman (1819-92) was one of America's most important poets, whose free verse *Leaves of Grass* celebrated America and the common people.

▼ Kurt Vonnegut (born 1922) is one of a new breed of young American authors whose books, like *Breakfast of Champions* have a large devoted following.

▲ Leonard Bernstein (born 1918) is a versatile musician who conducted the New York Philharmonic and composed both symphonic and stage music.

▶ Film-making combines many arts, as in the creation of this outdoor setting for the production of the film *Lord Jim*.

Reaching for the sky

Whitney and the vital cotton gin

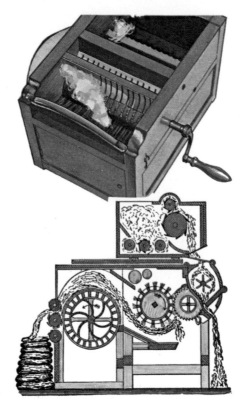

▲ Eli Whitney, the son of a well-to-do farmer, invented the cotton gin in 1793. But his great fortune was made later in the firearms business. This portrait is by Samuel Morse, who later perfected telegraphy.

▲ Before Whitney, cotton fibre had to be separated from the seed by hand. Some say the cotton gin helped cause the Civil War, because without it, slavery would have been unprofitable, and might have been ended.

Edison—lighting up the world

Thomas Alva Edison has been called the greatest inventor in history. His first patent, in 1868 was for an electric vote counter. This was followed by 63 years of creative work leading to the electric light, the phonograph, the stock ticker, the motion picture camera and projector, the storage battery, the dictating machine, the telephone transmitter and much more.

Great steps in communication

A very early Bell telephone

Alexander Graham Bell was born in Scotland, but in his twenties he moved to New England as a teacher of the deaf. In 1876, he perfected his telephone, and within ten years he was a famous and wealthy man. He is shown here making the first telephone call between New York and Chicago. The telephone has come a long way since Bell. Now many American businessmen carry portable wireless telephones around with them in their briefcases.

The birth of flight

Orville and Wilbur Wright, two young brothers who owned a bicycle shop, became interested in flight in 1896. After seven years of research and experiment, they built their first aeroplane, and on December 17, 1903, on the beach at Kitty Hawk, North Carolina, it flew on the first attempt, just as the Wright Brothers were certain it would.

Edison's electric lamp 1879

The first recording machine 1877

The race to the moon

▶ Robert H. Goddard, a physicist, was the first person to conduct serious research with rockets, in 1909. His first liquid fuel rocket was launched in 1926. But he received little encouragement from the government, which did not pursue rocket research in earnest until after World War II, with the aid of many German scientists. Rocket science reached a peak when Apollo 11 (right) carried the first men to the moon.

▲ In 1961, President John Kennedy set a goal "of landing a man on the moon and returning him safely to earth" by the end of the decade. NASA, the National Aeronautics and Space Administration, met this goal with five months to spare. Due to budget cuts, no more moon flights are scheduled for this century. Instead, NASA will concentrate on its reusable space shuttle and on unmanned space probes to other planets.

Cars for the masses

Henry Ford built his first motor car in 1896. By 1914 his Ford Motor Company was very successful, and profits were being shared with all employees. Ford introduced the concept of the assembly line, which revolutionized production methods, and made the Model T, in "any colour you want as long as it's black", America's most popular automobile.

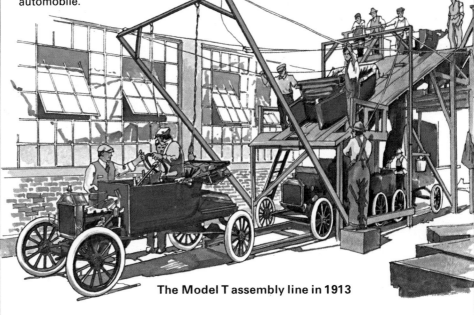

The Model T assembly line in 1913

Customs and superstitions

Days for celebration

Americans do enjoy holidays, if only as an excuse for a party. There are no national holidays; each state chooses its own. So while all states celebrate Christmas, Washington's birthday, Labor Day, Independence Day and Thanksgiving, there are dozens of holidays celebrated in anywhere from one state (All Saints Day, Louisiana) to 40 states (Christopher Columbus Day).

The 4th of July is a major celebration day, commemorating the signing of the Declaration of Independence in 1776. Most towns have parades during the day and firework displays in the evening.

Thanksgiving is celebrated on the fourth Thursday in November in memory of the feast the Pilgrims had after their first harvest in 1621. The usual meal is turkey with chestnut stuffing, sweet potatoes, and both pumpkin and mince pies.

At Christmas, many people decorate the outsides of their houses in spectacular fashion: dummy Santa Clauses coming down the chimney, life-size creches on the lawn, even artificial snow in warmer climates.

The Congress, at the request of special interest groups, regularly declares National Days or Weeks including, for example, National Dog Week, Pickle Week, Library Week, Popcorn Farmers Day, and Humor Week. No one takes these too seriously.

American superstitions

Many Americans are quite superstitious, although they may deny it publicly (probably crossing their fingers as they do so!) Many tall buildings have no thirteenth floor. People on the fourteenth floor know it really is the thirteenth, but it makes them feel better to pretend it is the fourteenth. Superstitions have come to America from the many different cultures that made up today's Americans, and this mixing of people has created specially American ones too.

▼ Rodeos originated as spare-time contests for cowboys, but have turned into a great national tradition. Many small towns stage their own, and large travelling rodeos are second in popularity only to circuses.

Some American superstitions

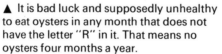

▲ So many Americans are worried by the number 13 that many buildings have no 13th floor; the builders think no one would want to live or work there.

▲ It is bad luck and supposedly unhealthy to eat oysters in any month that does not have the letter "R" in it. That means no oysters four months a year.

▲ When you see a hay truck or wagon, you can make one wish. But if you happen to see the same hay again, the wish won't come true.

▲ It is very important that you never step on a crack in the sidewalk, for if you do, it is very likely to cause your mother a broken back.

▲ In Pennsylvania, the Amish people practise a fundamental religion. This Amish man at his bank is unhappy because he believes he has committed a sin by being photographed.

▲ On Hallowe'en, children dress up in costumes and go "trick or treating" from door to door. If they aren't given a treat, they play a trick, like soaping up the windows. Carved pumpkins, or jack-o-lanterns, with candles inside decorate many homes.

▶ The major political parties select their candidates for President and Vice President at huge political conventions, with delegates from all states. Conventions are usually about half carnival and half very serious business.

The mobile Americans

Where the car is king

American trains are awful, planes good, buses are very good, but automobiles still reign supreme. There are over 100 million passenger cars, an average of nearly two per family. There are 115 million licenced drivers, who use their cars for about 90 per cent of all holiday trips. Much of this is on the nearly-completed interstate highway system, 68,000 kilometres (42,500 miles) of four to twelve lane motorways connecting every state in the union except Alaska and Hawaii.

Most states issue driver's licences at age 16, but 14 year olds can often get licences to drive only to and from school.

The Federal government took over the passenger carrying railroads in 1971, but the service has improved only a little. Passenger miles travelled have dropped by more than half since 1960, and there is still talk of ending all inter-city traffic.

A thousand bus companies operate nearly 25,000 inter-city buses, serving nearly every city, town and village in America. Many of these huge coaches have toilets, and even stewardesses who serve meals *en route*.

But distances in America are so great that airlines are becoming a very popular form of travel. More than fifty national and regional airline companies serve over 1,000 airports with jumbo jets, small "commuter planes" and large passenger helicopters.

Postal and telephone networks

The American telephone system is privately owned. More than a hundred separate companies, all linked together, provide the best service in the world. Many cities have push-button phones, and some have videophone service, where you can see the person as well as talk. And the service is cheap. At night you can call coast to coast—about 3,000 miles—for about 10p a minute.

The postal service is often thought to be as bad as the phones are good. There is one delivery a day, sometimes only in the late afternoon.

▲ These huge inter-city buses have toilets and stewardesses, and frequently cover 1600 kilometres or more in a single day.

◄ The passenger-carrying functions of American railroads were nationalized in 1971 under the name of Amtrak.

The many airlines of the U.S.A.

PAN AM

TWA

United Air Lines

DELTA ®

A'A
American Airlines

BI
BRANIFF INTERNATIONAL
U.S. MAINLAND HAWAII MEXICO SOUTH AMERICA

EASTERN AIRLINES

▲ Americans make nearly 200 million airplane trips a year on dozens of scheduled airlines and helicopter services. Busy airports may be served by 30 or more airlines averaging over 1000 flights a day.

▼ Huge passenger-carrying helicopters can take off and land on the heliport atop the 59-storey PanAm building in the heart of New York City. Many people have objected to the noise and the possible dangers.

▲ There are over 120 million vehicles in America, and sometimes it seems as if they are all on the same road at the same time.

◄ New York is North America's largest and busiest port. Major ocean liners, both passenger and cargo, can actually dock within four blocks of Times Square in the heart of central Manhattan.

Chicago
an American city

The wagon camp that grew

America has no single great city, as many countries do: London, Paris, Stockholm, Tokyo, and others. All America's outstanding cities—New York, San Francisco, Houston, Washington, Seattle—are very American, yet very different from each other. In many ways, however, Chicago may be the most typical of all.

In the 1830s, Chicago was a small camp for wagons on the way west. By 1871, when the heart of the city was destroyed by fire there were 300,000 residents. Today there are nearly 3.5 million, with 4 million more in the surrounding suburbs.

Chicago is a great manufacturing centre, leading the nation in producing steel, television sets, appliances, meat products, musical instruments, and much else. But the city has paid the price. Lake Michigan, on whose shores it is built, is badly polluted, and many beaches have been closed.

The Chicagoans

Many of Chicago's citizens live in detached single-family houses, but there are huge public housing skyscrapers as well. The city has numerous ethnic neighbourhoods, where the stores, churches, and lifestyles reflect the Polish, Italian, Chinese, Swedish and other backgrounds of the people.

Chicagoans are fiercely divided as to whether they support the White Sox or the Cubs baseball teams, but they unite behind the Bears (football) and Black Hawks (hockey).

The grand scale of Chicago

Tens of thousands of commuters come into Chicago on double-deck trains each morning, to work in some of the tallest and most unusual buildings in the world. Countless others drive their own cars, creating massive traffic jams on the eight-lane motorways leading into the city.

The Chicago area has seven major universities, the world's largest and busiest commercial airport, and thanks to the St. Lawrence Seaway, it has an ocean port 900 miles from the sea.

▲ The Chicago area is truly a melting pot of races, religions and national backgrounds. There are more Jews than in Jerusalem, more Blacks than in Nairobi, and tens of thousands each of Irish-Americans, German-Americans, Polish-Americans, British-Americans, Italian-Americans, and Mexican-Americans, all living together in relative harmony.

▲ Prohibition brought about rapid growth of organized crime, supplying beer and whiskey to Americans. Chicago was the centre of mobsterism with the infamous Al Capone (above) as the chief gangster.

◄ Chicagoans tolerated the city's many gangland murders because, as one gangster said, "We only kill each other."

◄ Chicago's skyline includes the Sears Tower (at 115 storeys, the world's tallest when built), the unusual twin round 50-storey Marina City blocks of flats (the bottom 17 floors are car parks), and the Chicago River, a direct link, via the St. Lawrence Seaway, to the distant Atlantic Ocean.

▲ Chicago's central shopping and business areas is called "The Loop" because it is surrounded by a loop of the elevated railway train. Madison Street is only a few blocks from Lake Michigan, and the brisk winds that blow from the Lake give Chicago its nickname, "The Windy City".

The native Americans

The Indian nations

In the last years of the ice age, about 20,000 years ago, there was a great migration of people from Asia, across a now-submerged land bridge to Alaska, and down into the Americas. Christopher Columbus called these people Indians, because he thought he had landed in India.

It is a mistake to think that all Indians are similar. One Indian nation could be as different from another as, say, Sweden is from Italy. Hundreds of tribes each had their own language, clothing, crafts, foods, and house styles.

An Iroquois in Massachusetts (more than half the U.S. states have Indian names) might live in a birchbark tent, wear a deerskin kilt, and shave his head. A Sioux of Nebraska would live in a buffalo-hide tipi, wear his hair in long braids, with the bravest chiefs entitled to wear a bonnet of coloured eagle feathers. And a Hopi of Arizona would weave his clothes from sheep's wool, and live in a kind of block of flats made of clay, called a pueblo.

Meeting the settlers

Indians were generally kind to the early European settlers, introducing them to chocolate, corn, peanuts and other foods. But the Europeans wanted the Indian's land, and more often than not, took it by force, pushing the Indians further and further west. Many tribes fought vigorously to retain or recapture their land, from the French and Indian Wars of the mid eighteenth century to the last battle, at Wounded Knee, South Dakota in 1890.

Indians were not granted full rights of citizenship until 1953. Even today, though the Indian population is increasing after years of decline (nearly 800,000 in 1970), unemployment and poverty among Indians is much greater than for other Americans. Militant young Indians have been campaigning for recognition of the Indian's problems—notably by sitting in on land they claim was illegally taken away from their forefathers.

▲ In 1876, General Custer was sent to Montana to defeat the Sioux, but the Indians, led by Crazy Horse, killed Custer and all his men.

▼ Indians of the Plains depended on the buffalo for food, clothing and shelter. Their tipis were made from 25 or 30 buffalo hides.

▲ Sitting Bull (1834?-1890) was a famous tribal leader and holy man of the Hunkpapa Sioux. After Little Big Horn, he escaped to Canada, later gave himself up, and after a prison term, travelled with Buffalo Bill's Circus.

Where the Indian tribes were found

Blackfoot

Sioux

Cree

Blackfoot

Chippewa

Crow

Mohawk
Iroquois
Susquehanna
Delaware

Sioux

Cheyenne

Illinois

Miwok

Paiute

Shawnee

Navajo

Kiowa

Cherokee

Osage

Chicksaw

Apache

Muskogee   Creek

Comanche   Wichita   Caddo   Choctaw

Apache

Kiowa

▲ Many of America's Indians today live on reservations in desert areas of the far west, such as these people in Monument Valley.

▼ In 1972, militant Indians conducted a "sit-in" at the Bureau of Indian Affairs in Washington to protest against discriminatory treatment.

Cowboys and the Wild West

A hard and lonely life

The cowboy's life seems glamorous and fun-filled, if we are to believe the thousands of western films made over the years. But in the days of the old west, and even today, the life of the cowboy was hard, lonely, often boring, and sometimes dangerous.

As America expanded into the wide open spaces of the west in the mid-1800s, cattle-raising became one of the main activities. Because the cattle might be spread out over miles of ranchland, men were needed to take care of them, to round up strays, and to bring the herd to market. These men came to be called cowhands, or cowboys.

Cowboys, then and now, often "ride herd" for days or weeks at a time. Normally, they live in bunkhouses on the ranch, but when out on the range, they frequently sleep under the stars, or in tents. They get their meals, then, from a chuckwagon, a sort of travelling kitchen on wheels.

Although many people think of cowboys as looking something like John Wayne, they come in all sizes, shapes, and even colours. Many Negroes, and even Japanese and Chinese worked as cowboys in the west.

The distinctive outfits worn by cowboys, their "sixguns", their many famous songs, and their supposedly glamorous life, have made cowboys heroes all over the world.

▲ The cowboy's distinctive outfit is chosen to keep him warm, safe and dry, as he performs many different chores in many kinds of weather. But not all cowboys wear the huge "ten gallon" felt hats.

▶ Dodge City, Kansas, used to be the wildest town in the west. It was the world's largest cattle market, and when the cowboys came to town, not even marshals Bat Masterson and Wyatt Earp could maintain law and order.

Outlaws of the west

Some people regard outlaws as folk heroes—a sort of American Robin Hood; others despise them as the cold-blooded killers and robbers many of them were. Among the best-known outlaws were these: Billy the Kid (right) who killed his first man at 12 and was finally gunned down by Sheriff Pat Garrett; the gang of Butch Cassidy and Harry Longbaugh, the Sundance Kid (below); Jesse and Frank James, who terrorized the West, robbing banks and trains; and the curious Black Bart, who left long, colourful poems behind when he robbed stage-coaches. Almost alone among outlaws, Black Bart served his time in prison and died peacefully, a free man.

▼ The Western film began in Hollywood, but soon gained popularity all over the world, along with their stars, like Tom Mix and William (Hopalong Cassidy) Boyd. Now Westerns are even made in Italy and Japan.

▲ Calamity Jane (Martha Jane Canarray) (1852?-1903) was a colourful figure of the Old West. She could ride, shoot and rope as well as most men. Many books, stories and songs have been written about her.

Benjamin Franklin and independence

The Crown and the colonists

After Great Britain acquired Canada from France in 1763, it began exercising more control over all its North American colonies. The colonists resented the ever-increasing taxes, especially since they were not represented in Parliament.

Despite the best efforts of Benjamin Franklin, who had spent 18 years in England helping settle problems arising between the Crown and the colonies, the colonists, under Patrick Henry's rallying cry of "Give me liberty or give me death" moved closer and closer to declaring their independence from England.

The British attempted to put down the colonists' uprising, but warned by Paul Revere's midnight ride, the Minutemen of Massachusetts defended themselves at Lexington and Concord in 1775, and two months later gave a good account of themselves at the Battle of Bunker Hill, Boston.

The American revolution

The Declaration of Independence was adopted on July 4, 1776, and the "Revolutionary War" was under way.

Franklin, then 70, returned from England to carry out half a dozen different jobs, from reorganizing General Washington's army to printing new paper money. He helped write the Declaration of Independence, and before signing it said, "We must all hang together or most assuredly we shall all hang separately."

In 1778, Franklin negotiated a treaty of aid with France, who provided money and troops. The British surrendered in 1781, and a new British cabinet recognized American independence in March 1782.

After the war, Franklin was sent to France as American Ambassador, returning a few years later to help write the American Constitution (1785-7).

The Constitution was adopted in 1788, and the following year George Washington was chosen to be the first President of the United States. Then, at 83, Franklin took up his last great cause, working for the abolition of slavery. He died in 1790.

▲ By flying a kite in a thunderstorm, Franklin proved that lightning was electrical in nature. Franklin always had a strong interest in science and invention; he is credited with inventing the lightning rod, bifocal eyeglasses, an improved harmonica, and a new kind of stove for the home.

The American colonies in 1763

Louisbourg
CANADA
New York
Fort Duquesne (Pittsburgh)
St. Louis
LOUISIANA
GEORGIA
FLORIDA
BAHAMAS
New Orleans
CUBA
MEXICO
JAMAICA

British territory
French territory
Spanish territory

▲ The hated British tax collectors were sometimes subjected to tar and feathering by irate colonists. Resisting the "Tea Act", colonists dumped a cargo of British tea into Boston Harbour, the "Boston Tea Party".

▲ In a surprise move on Christmas Day 1776, General George Washington and his troops crossed the Delaware River, and won a first decisive victory at Trenton, New Jersey.

▼ The Declaration of Independence, written by Thomas Jefferson, guaranteeing every man the right to ''Life, Liberty and the Pursuit of Happiness'' was signed on July 4, 1776.

▼ One of the most famous battles of the War of Independence occurred at Bunker Hill, in Boston. Twice, 1000 colonists drove off 3000 British troops, but finally the colonials retreated before the ''redcoats''.

Abraham Lincoln the fight for union

The lawyer from Indiana

Abraham Lincoln, the sixteenth president of the United States is regarded by many Americans as one of the great heroes in the nation's history.

Born in a log cabin, Lincoln grew up in the states of Indiana and Illinois. After his election to the Illinois state assembly (1834), Lincoln began to study law, and made his first public statements opposing slavery, because it is "founded on both injustice and bad policy".

After one term in the national Congress, Lincoln returned to Illinois, where his law firm prospered.

The Civil War

In 1856 he helped found a new political party in Illinois, the Republicans. In 1860 the Republicans chose him as their presidential candidate. The opposing Democratic party was badly divided on the slavery question, and Lincoln was elected easily.

Extremists from southern states had threatened to withdraw from the union if Lincoln were elected, and by the day he took office, seven states had seceded to form the Confederate States of America.

When the southern army captured a government fort in South Carolina, Lincoln called out the militia, and the Civil War had, in effect, begun.

Lincoln strongly felt his most important goal was to preserve the union. In 1862 he issued the Emancipation Proclamation, which freed the slaves in a few states, and paved the way for the Thirteenth Amendment to the Constitution, outlawing all slavery.

The assassination of Lincoln

One week after southern general Robert E. Lee surrendered to northern general Ulysses S. Grant, Abraham Lincoln was shot by an actor, John Wilkes Booth, and died the following morning.

▲ When Abraham Lincoln was elected President, he had no beard, as in this photograph by Matthew Brady. But a little girl wrote to Lincoln that she thought he would look better with a beard, so he grew one!

Who fought whom in the Civil War

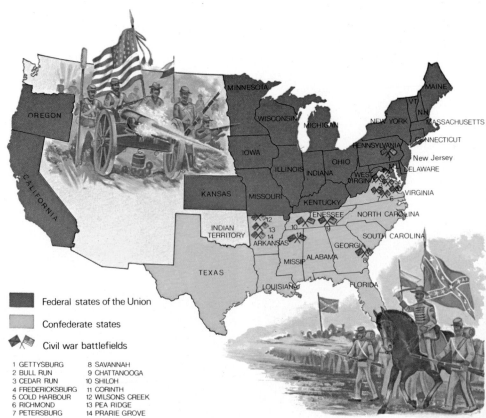

■ Federal states of the Union

■ Confederate states

⚔ Civil war battlefields

1 GETTYSBURG	8 SAVANNAH
2 BULL RUN	9 CHATTANOOGA
3 CEDAR RUN	10 SHILOH
4 FREDERICKSBURG	11 CORINTH
5 COLD HARBOUR	12 WILSONS CREEK
6 RICHMOND	13 PEA RIDGE
7 PETERSBURG	14 PRARIE GROVE

◀ In 1861 and 1862, the South appeared to be winning the war. But the North's victory at the Battle of Gettysburg (June 1863) turned the tide in favour of the Union.

▼ The American Civil War was one of the bloodiest wars in history. Nearly one fourth of the 2.2 million participants died, and hundreds of thousands more were wounded. Many fell to these Union guns at Fort Brady, Virginia.

▲ Five days after Lee surrendered to Grant, effectively ending the Civil War, President Lincoln was shot to death while attending a play at Ford's Theater in Washington. His assassin, a well-known actor named John Wilkes Booth, was killed a fortnight later, and four other conspirators were later hanged. Millions of Americans lined the tracks as Lincoln's funeral train carried his body home to Springfield, Illinois.

▲ The Lincoln Memorial in Washington is visited by millions of people every year. The heroic statue of Lincoln meditating is by Daniel French, completed in 1922.

Martin Luther King man of peace

▲ King led many protest marches for racial equality and civil rights in the South.

The second-class citizens

The civil war had effects on America that can still be seen and felt today—but things are changing in some ways. The freed slaves who remained in the South (and many in the North as well) were regarded as second-class citizens, often having to attend segregated (all black) schools, and even being required to use separate toilets and drinking fountains.

In 1954, the U.S. Supreme Court ruled that "separate but equal" schools for blacks and whites were unconstitutional, and that schools must begin to integrate with "all deliberate speed".

After this, black leaders began to emerge, capable of winning the support of many persons, black and white. Foremost among these was the Rev. Martin Luther King, pastor of a Baptist church in Atlanta, Georgia, and a strong advocate of nonviolent demonstrations for change.

The march on Washington

Dissatisfied with the pace of desegregation, in 1963 Dr. King led more than 200,000 persons in a march on Washington in support of equal rights for all. King said, "I have a dream that this nation will rise up and live out the true meaning of its creed, 'we hold these truths to be self-evident that all men are created equal'."

President John F. Kennedy, himself a strong believer in equal rights for all, met King; and at the time of Kennedy's assassination later the same year, he had been working for the passage of a new, strong civil rights law in America.

In 1968, Martin Luther King was killed by a sniper's bullet in a Tennessee motel room. His murderer was caught; conspiracy was suspected, but nothing was proved.

Twenty years after the Supreme Court desegregation decision, most schools are integrated, but black leaders in America say there is some distance to go before Martin Luther King's dream comes true. New people lead, sometimes using new methods, but the old struggle continues.

▼ Despite all the efforts of social reformers and well-meaning politicians, many millions of Americans still go to bed hungry every night and live in dismal slum conditions.

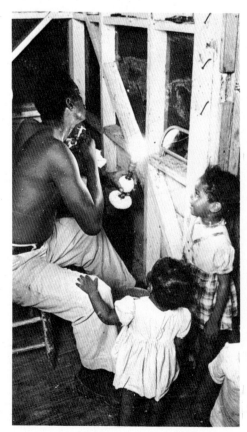

▲ Martin Luther King believed in the peaceful resistance philosophy of Mahatma Gandhi. King himself has inspired many activities for

▲ The Ku Klux Klan was organized in the South in the 19th century to terrorize Negroes. It has been revived in recent years. Members wear white robes and pointed hats.

peace ranging from restaurant sit-ins for integration to this New York march to protest against the war in Vietnam.

▲ A crucial moment in school integration occurred in 1957 when Governor Faubus of Arkansas ordered state troops to prevent Negroes from enrolling in Little Rock's Central High School. President Eisenhower in turn ordered Federal troops to escort the nine blacks to class. Today the school, like many in the South, is fully integrated.

▼ Riots by inner city blacks erupted in many American cities between the summers of 1965 and 1968. Here, in Detroit, at least 40 died, and thousands were left homeless by fires. The Kerner Commission Report on the causes of these riots said that white racism was the leading cause, with unemployment and frustration as leading factors.

Heroes of fact and fiction

Folk heroes

America has many folk heroes. Some are real, some are purely fictional, and quite a few are real people on whom legends have been built, until it is hard to know what is true and what is not.

For example, Paul Revere was a real man who rode through the night to warn the colonists that the British were coming. But it was not until Longfellow wrote a stirring poem many years later ("Listen my children and you shall hear of the midnight ride of Paul Revere . . .") that he became a true hero.

Even Paul Bunyan, the legendary giant lumberjack who could level a forest with one blow of his axe, and who dug the Mississippi River when his ox grew thirsty, may well have been based on a real, if smaller person.

There are many heroes of the wild west, most of them are real: Wild Bill Hickok; Buffalo Bill; Annie Oakley, the greatest pistol shot ever; and Wyatt Earp, the lawman who won the gunfight at OK Corral and died peacefully 50 years later. Indian heroes include the great warriors Crazy Horse and Sitting Bull, and Pocahontas, the chief's daughter who saved the life of an Englishman, Captain John Smith.

Today's heroes

The Astronauts are heroes to many Americans, especially the first man in orbit, John Glenn, and the first man on the moon, Neil Armstrong.

Most Sunday newspapers have many pages of colour comics, and there are a lot of "funny book heroes" for child and adult alike: Charlie Brown and Snoopy, Pogo the Possum, detective Dick Tracy, hillbilly Li'l Abner, and inept solder Beetle Bailey are popular.

Pop music stars are heroes to many, though they come and go quite rapidly. But Bob Dylan, Elvis Presley, Glenn Campbell, Joan Baez, and Simon & Garfunkel are among those who have been popular for many years.

▲ A real man, John Chapman (1755?-1847) is celebrated in legends as Johnny Appleseed. Chapman devoted his life to walking all over the Midwest planting apple trees, a friend to pioneer and Indian alike. Many songs and ballads have been written of him.

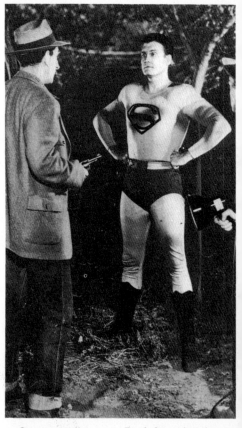

▲ Superman "came to Earth from the planet Krypton to fight crime and injustice" in the 1930s, and has remained a popular comic strip hero since then.

◄ Generations of children have been frightened out of their wits by Washington Irving's *Legend of Sleepy Hollow* in which the superstitious schoolmaster Ichabod Crane disappears after an encounter with the Headless Horseman of Sleepy Hollow.

1. PEANUTS

3. DO YOU BELIEVE IN FREEDOM, BIG BROTHER? OF COURSE...I'M A GREAT BELIEVER IN FREEDOM..

4. THAT'S GOOD BECAUSE YOUR BEACH BALL JUST WON ITS FREEDOM!

▲ New York City honours American heroes with an unusual custom, the ticker tape parade. The hero astronauts, athletes and soldiers, ride along in open cars while people throw vast quantities of paper from windows.

▲ The Peanuts comic strip, drawn by Charles Schulz, is the most popular in America. Millions of people look forward to the daily adventures of Charlie Brown, Snoopy, Linus, Lucy and their friends.

▼ Elvis Presley, an unknown folk singer from Tupelo, Mississippi, suddenly shot to stardom in 1956 as the first great rock and roll idol. Many have followed his path, but after nearly 20 years, Elvis still has hundreds of fan clubs and millions of fans.

▲ John F. Kennedy has become a hero to many Americans. The youngest elected President had a mystique, a style that generated hero worship, and his murder in 1963 is a black mark on American history.

49

The American character

The friendly optimists

Americans like to think of themselves as being friendly and open. To a large extent they are—though still a little suspicious of foreigners. They feel the American way of life is surely the best in the world, and cannot understand why other countries don't always think so.

Most people believe America can survive any crisis. After all, it has never lost a war, never been bombed or invaded, and everything will work out somehow. This applies equally to graft, corruption, and environmental pollution.

Americans will tolerate almost anything, ideologically, from Ku Klux Klan cross burnings to Black Panther rallies. But when his own life is affected, the American will complain and protest vigorously until he gets what he wants. They believe they can change the system. The positive results achieved, from the civil rights sit-ins to Ralph Nader's effect on auto safety laws, show they are sometimes right.

Only a few generations removed from the pioneers, many still think they have that spirit, and could clear 40 acres, build a house and track a bear—if only they felt like it!

▲ Most people try to be friendly with everyone. Complete strangers will be on a Christian-name basis shortly after they meet.

▲ Americans are proud of their ethnic backgrounds, but also proud to be Americans. Buttons and flags are worn a great deal.

▲ Many people have a grandparent or great-grandparent who was a pioneer, and they see themselves as still carrying on some element of the old west and the pioneer spirit.

▲ They like to think of themselves as a little bit individualistic, even if most homes, cars and suits look pretty much the same.

◀ Many people like to think of the Osmond family as typical Americans: well-scrubbed, religious, handsome, loyal—and rich.

▲ Americans are proud of industrial "know-how" symbolized by Henry Ford's invention of the assembly line method of manufacturing.

▲ Americans like to think they have always done the best or bravest thing through history. Children learn that America won the War of 1812; others disagree. The Alamo, a massive defeat of the Texans by the Mexicans, is typically shown here as just the opposite.

◀ Americans are proud of their revolutionary heritage, and put it on display at restored villages like Williamsburg, Virginia.

▼ The Constitution gives the "right to bear arms", and for millions of Americans this is a sacred privilege. Many homes have guns, and all policemen carry at least one.

How the United States is changing

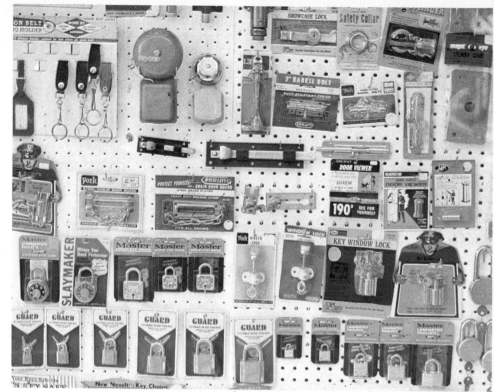

Living standards

Most American cities actually lost population between 1960 and 1970 as the richer whites moved out to the suburbs and poorer blacks moved to the inner cities. Washington, Baltimore and Atlanta are now more than 50 per cent black.

America is making slow progress in closing the immense gap between rich and poor. In 1959, 39 million people lived in poverty. In 1970 it was still 27 million, about a third either black or of Spanish origin. But the median family income was above $10,000 (£4,700) for the first time in history, in the 1970 census.

People are becoming better educated. Between 1960 and 1970, the percentage of children finishing high school rose from 65 to 79 per cent.

American life expectancy has increased dramatically, from 47 years in 1900 to nearly 70 now. Four per cent of the population were "senior citizens" in 1900; now it is over 10 per cent.

Looking to the future

Although many city dwellers have a dream of "getting back to the land", the number of farmers has dropped almost alarmingly. There were nearly seven million farms in 1935; there are less than three million today.

As recently as the 1950s, American women averaged more than 3.5 children each. But on the momentous day of December 4, 1972, the U.S. achieved zero population growth—a figure just over 2 children per family. Some experts now believe the population may decline over the next few decades.

Americans are continuing to take much greater interest in the forces that shape their lives: the environment, the health of the people (the U.S.A. is the only western nation with no national health care programme). And the Watergate scandals of recent years have increased political awareness of most Americans in generally healthy ways.

▲ America is a violent country, that unfortunately seems to be growing more violent all the time. There are over 2,000 violent crimes, including 50 murders, on the average, every *day*. Americans are becoming very security-conscious. City dwellers often have four or five locks on their doors and a vicious dog (or at least a tape recording of one snarling) standing by inside.

▼ The U.S. and China had been at odds ever since the communists gained control in 1949. But a new era in international diplomacy began in February 1972 with President Nixon's visit to Peking, where he had cordial meetings with Chairman Mao.

▲ Many Americans, including these veterans on a peace march, used to think of wars as noble efforts to bring "The American Way of Life" to the rest of the world. But Vietnam changed all that; America is less likely to become involved in other nations' affairs.

▼ Americans are never shy to announce where they stand on given issues, often through lapel buttons and bumper stickers. Minority groups, like Chicanos (Mexican-Americans) are developing racial pride, and political awareness extends to the youngest children.

▲ In the early 1970s, America was rocked by the worst scandals in the nation's history. They are known as the Watergate Affair, because in 1972, Republican spies were caught breaking into Democratic party offices in the Watergate building. Investigation of this crime led to discovery of many crimes committed by high-ranking Republicans: burglary, bribery, extortion, perjury, and much more. Dozens of powerful officials, including cabinet officers and Vice President Agnew resigned under pressure; many of these were indicted and convicted of their crimes. The climax came in 1974, with the inauguration of impeachment proceedings against President Richard M. Nixon.

▶ In the 1960s, few people worried about the environment. Now nearly everyone does. Tough new laws make it harder for factories like this to be operated; all cars are fitted with anti-pollution devices, and cleaner air and water has become an important national goal.

Reference
Physical and Human Geography

Facts and figures

Position: North America, between Atlantic and Pacific Oceans; Canadian and Mexican borders; Alaska north-west of Canada; Hawaii in mid-Pacific ocean.
Area: 9,363,000 square kilometres.
Population: (1972) 208,837,000.
Capital: Washington, District of Columbia.
Languages: American English; Hawaiian, Creole, many Indian languages.
Religion: 23% Roman Catholic, 13% Baptist, 6% Methodist, 4% Lutheran, 3% Jewish, 14% others, 37% no affiliation.
The State: Independence declared 1776, recognized 1782 (thirteen original states). 50th (last) state admitted, 1959.
International organizations: Some cooperative organizations the U.S. belongs to are the United Nations, the North Atlantic Treaty Organization, the Organization of American States, and the Southeast Asia Treaty Organization.

The climate of the U.S.A.

The U.S. is so large, there can be no common weather characteristics. On the same day, one state may be 60°C. colder than another. The southern states generally have mild winters and hot summers. The midwest and northern states have very cold winters, but also often have hot summers. Normal rainfall varies from 17 cm. a year in parts of the southwest to more than 170 cm. a year in parts of the deep south.

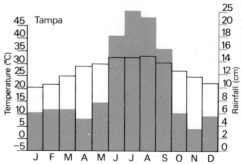

New York

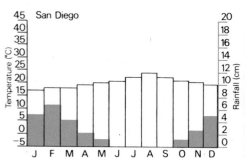

Tampa

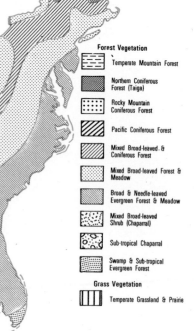

San Diego

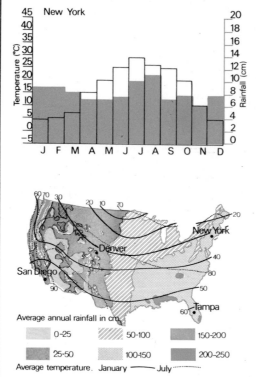

Average annual rainfall in cm.

- 0-25
- 25-50
- 50-100
- 100-150
- 150-200
- 200-250

Average temperature. January —— July ············

The natural vegetation of the U.S.A.

Desert Vegetation

Semi-desert & Mesquite Grassland

Desert, Sage & Brush

Forest Vegetation
- Temperate Mountain Forest
- Northern Coniferous Forest (Taiga)
- Rocky Mountain Coniferous Forest
- Pacific Coniferous Forest
- Mixed Broad-leaved & Coniferous Forest
- Mixed Broad-leaved Forest & Meadow
- Broad & Needle-leaved Evergreen Forest & Meadow
- Mixed Broad-leaved Shrub (Chaparral)
- Sub-tropical Chaparral
- Swamp & Sub-tropical Evergreen Forest

Grass Vegetation
- Temperate Grassland & Prairie

Major towns of the U.S.A.

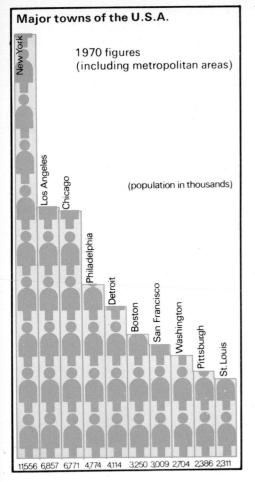

1970 figures
(including metropolitan areas)

(population in thousands)

New York — 11,556
Los Angeles — 6,857
Chicago — 6,771
Philadelphia — 4,774
Detroit — 4,114
Boston — 3,250
San Francisco — 3,009
Washington — 2,704
Pittsburgh — 2,386
St. Louis — 2,311

The population density

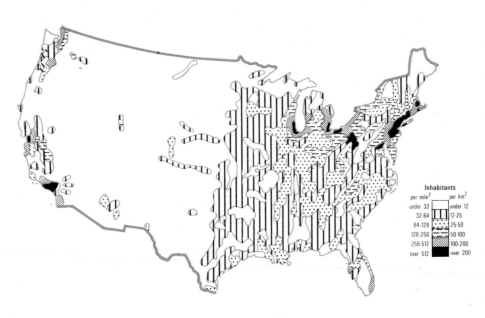

Inhabitants

per mile²	per km²
under 32	under 12
32-64	12-25
64-128	25-50
128-256	50-100
256-512	100-200
over 512	over 200

The population picture

The population of the United States is very unevenly distributed across the land. Nearly three-fourths of the people (73·5%) live on 1·5% of the land. Population density ranges from ·5 person per square mile (Alaska) to more than 12,000 per square mile (District of Columbia). Besides this trend from rural to urban living, there has been, for many years, a move from south to north, and from east to west. The population centre in 1790 (when there were 3·9 million Americans) was east of Baltimore, near the east coast. By 1970 it had moved to Illinois, nearly 1,000 miles west.

How the U.S.A. is governed

The Federal (national) government is divided into three branches, the executive (President, etc.), legislative (Senate and House of Representatives) and judicial (the courts). The Constitution provides for "checks and balances" among these three branches. The legislative branch makes the laws, which must be signed by the President, but can be passed over his veto (refusal to sign) by a two-thirds majority vote. The Supreme Court may reject unconstitutional laws. Supreme Court judges, ambassadors, and other Federal officials are chosen by the President, but must be approved by the Senate. The House may vote to impeach (bring to trial) a President, who is then tried by the Senate with the Chief Justice presiding. He can be removed from office by a two-thirds vote of the Senators.

Each of the 50 states elects two Senators and from 1—43 Congressmen, depending on its population. Senators serve six years, Congressmen two years. The President and Vice President are elected for four years.

Each state has a Governor; most have a Lieutenant Governor. There are two legislative bodies in 49 states: a House and a Senate. (Nebraska has only one body.)

Counties are generally governed by Boards of Supervisors and policed by sheriffs. Cities have either elected mayors or hired city managers.

The system of government

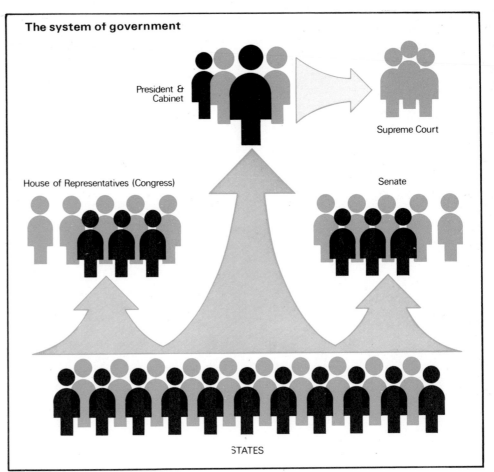

President & Cabinet

Supreme Court

House of Representatives (Congress)

Senate

STATES

Reference
History

Main events in U.S. History

Pre-historic times	Indians cross from Asia, settle throughout Americas
c.700–c.1000	Vikings, including Leif Erikson, visit American coast
1492	Christopher Columbus, Italian sailing for Spain, "discovers" America
1493–1610	Explorations by Cabot, Drake, Hudson, Raleigh (English), Cartier (French), Ponce de Leon (Spanish), others
1607	First permanent settlement, Jamestown, Virginia
1620	Pilgrims land in Mayflower to settle in New England
1620s to 1750s	British, French, Dutch, Spanish, others colonize eastern, south-western America
1636	Harvard University founded
1676	First major war with Indians; New England
1704	First newspaper, *Boston News Letter*
1752	Ben Franklin flies kite in thunder-storm; proves lightning is electricity
1754	War between British versus French and Indians
1773	Boston Tea Party to protest against British taxes
1775	Paul Revere's ride; Battle of Bunker Hill
1775–82	War of Independence, versus Great Britain
1776	Declaration of Independence signed, Philadelphia, July
1783	First state, Massachusetts, outlaws slavery
1787	Constitution written, Philadelphia
1789	George Washington chosen first president
1803	Jefferson's Louisiana purchase vastly expands America
1812	War of 1812, with British; city of Washington burned
1831	Nat Turner Rebellion, major slave uprising
1841	First wagon train of pioneers heads west
1846–8	Mexican War; Texas, California, five other states ceded to U.S.
1848	Gold discovered in California; great rush westward begins
1861–5	Civil War, between the Union (north) and Confederacy (south)
1865	President Abraham Lincoln assassinated
1869	Transcontinental railroad completed
1876	Indians' last great victory, defeating Custer's cavalry at Little Big Horn
1890	Battle of Wounded Knee; last major battle with Indians
1891	Edison patents first cinema device
1898–1900	Spanish-American War; U.S. acquires Puerto Rico, Philippines
1903	Wright Brothers' first airplane flight, North Carolina
1906	San Francisco destroyed by earthquake and fire
1917	U.S. enters World War I
1920	Prohibition makes all liquor illegal in America
1926	Robert Goddard demonstrates first liquid fuel rocket, Massachusetts
1927	Charles Lindbergh flies first solo flight across Atlantic
1929	Stock market crash; start of great depression
1933	Prohibition ends. Franklin Roosevelt becomes president
1941	U.S. enters World War II after bombing of Pearl Harbour, Hawaii
1945	Atomic bombs dropped on Japan; World War II ends
1950–3	Korean War
1951	First coast-to-coast television broadcast
1954	Racial segregation in schools ruled unconstitutional by Supreme Court
1958	First U.S. space satellite
1960	Sit-ins begin civil rights movement in south; John Kennedy elected president
1962	John Glenn becomes first American in space
1963	John Kennedy assassinated, Dallas, Texas
1964–73	U.S. involvement in Vietnam war
1969	Astronaut Neil Armstrong sets foot on the moon
1971	Voting age lowered from 21 to 18
1972	President Nixon visits China and Russia
1972–	Watergate political scandals

The War of Independence

1763	Great Britain acquires Canada from France; increases taxes and duties throughout North American colonies
1770	All duties except tea tax repealed; colonial unrest leads to Boston massacre
1775	Samuel Adams and Patrick Henry unite patriot leaders; call for liberty. First battles at Lexington and Concord. George Washington named Commander in Chief
1776	Continental Congress in June drafts Declaration of Independence; adopted July 4. Washington crosses Delaware; major victory
1777	Washington defeats Cornwallis at Princeton; army spends difficult winter at Valley Forge; Lafayette arrives
1778	France recognizes U.S. independence
1779	John Paul Jones wins sea battles
1780	Col. Benedict Arnold found to be British spy; escapes, becomes British General
1781	Thousands of French troops arrive to help Americans. Cornwallis retreats into South, surrenders on October 19
1782	British cabinet recognizes independence
1783	Washington orders army disbanded; he retires to Mount Vernon
1786	Congress calls convention to meet in Philadelphia to draft Constitution
1787	Constitution adopted at Convention; George Washington presiding
1789	Washington unanimously chosen first President, John Adams Vice-President; Supreme Court created by First Congress

The Civil War

1861	Six states form the Confederate States of America; five more join later. South Carolina demands surrender of Fort Sumter; U.S. troops refuse. South captures fort in first battle, April 12. Lincoln calls for 75,000 troops. Robert E. Lee resigns from U.S. Army to head the Confederate Army of Virginia. South wins major battles at Bull Run, Wilson's Creek, elsewhere
1862	Johnston (C.S.A.) surprises Grant (U.S.A.) at Shiloh; Johnston killed. Major ship battle between Monitor (U.S.A.) which sank Merrimack (C.S.A.). South continues to do well as major battles fought at Antietam, Gaines Mill, Frayser's Farm, Fredericksburg, etc.
1863	Emancipation Proclamation frees three million slaves in south. Lee, with 76,000 troops, invades north, but suffers major defeat at Gettysburg. Lincoln's "Gettysburg Address" at dedication of cemetery several months later. North wins major battle at Vicksburg
1864	Ulysses S. Grant made general in chief for north. Major battles with Lee's troops. Sherman's march to the sea devastates much of Georgia
1865	North invades South Carolina; General Custer wins major battle. Lee surrenders to Grant at Appomattox Court House, Virginia April 9. Lincoln assassinated April 14. Slavery abolished by 13th. Amendment to the Constitution December 18
1871	Court awards U.S. $15 million damages from Great Britain for damage done by British-equipped warships during civil war.

The Presidents of the United States

1. George Washington (1732–99) military hero; "Father of his country"
2. John Adams (1735–1826) Washington's Vice President
3. Thomas Jefferson (1743–1826) architect; scholar; wrote Declaration of Independence
4. James Madison (1751–1836) helped write the Constitution
5. James Monroe (1758–1831) opposed European colonization of Americas
6. John Quincy Adams (1767–1848) John Adams's son; opposed slavery
7. Andrew Jackson (1767–1836) "Old Hickory"
8. Martin Van Buren (1782–1862) "The Little Magician"; a superb politician
9. William Henry Harrison (1773–1841) Caught fatal pneumonia at inauguration
10. John Tyler (1790–1862)
11. James Polk (1795–1849) declared Mexican war; expansionist policies
12. Zachary Taylor (1784–1850) Mexican war hero
13. Millard Fillmore (1800–74)
14. Franklin Pierce (1804–69) Mexican war hero; pro-slavery policies
15. James Buchanan (1791–1868) only bachelor President; pro-slavery policies
16. Abraham Lincoln (1809–65) The Great Emancipator; hero of the common man
17. Andrew Johnson (1808–75) unlettered politician; impeached but not convicted
18. Ulysses S. Grant (1822–85) Civil War hero; reformed the civil service
19. Rutherford Hayes (1822–93)
20. James Garfield (1831–81) Civil War hero; professor; was assassinated
21. Chester Arthur (1830–86)
22. Grover Cleveland (1837–1908) reform candidate. Elected twice
23. Benjamin Harrison (1833–1901) Grandson of ninth president
24. William McKinley (1843–1901) declared war on Spain; assassinated
25. Theodore Roosevelt (1858–1919) war hero, big game hunter
26. William Howard Taft (1857–1930) college professor and Chief Justice
27. Woodrow Wilson (1856–1924) helped negotiate 1918 peace
28. Warren Harding (1865–1923) small-town newspaperman
29. Calvin Coolidge (1872–1933) "Silent Cal"
30. Herbert Hoover (1874–1964) mining engineer; 60 years in public service
31. Franklin D. Roosevelt (1882–1945) elected four times; "New Deal" reforms
32. Harry Truman (1884–1973) unexpected 1948 victory; surprisingly effective
33. Dwight D. Eisenhower (1890–1969) military hero; generally innocuous
34. John F. Kennedy (1917–63) youngest elected President; assassinated
35. Lyndon Johnson (1908–73) many social reforms; escalated Vietnam war
36. Richard Nixon (1913–) detente with Russia, China; Watergate scandals

The Arts

Writers

Louisa May Alcott (1832–88) author of *Little Women*, social reformer

Horatio Alger (1832–99) wrote hundreds of popular books for boys

James Baldwin (1924–) black novelist, journalist, *The Far Country*

Stephen Vincent Benet (1898–1943) poet, novelist, *John Brown's Body*

Pearl Buck (1892–) Nobel prize winner, *The Good Earth*

Edgar Rice Burroughs (1875–1950) Tarzan adventure stories and books

Rachel Carson (1907–64) marine biologist and author, *The Silent Spring*

Saul Bellow (1915–) novelist, *Herzog*

James Fenimore Cooper (1789–1851) novelist, *Last of Mohicans*

E. E. Cummings (1894–1963) poet; known for eccentric typography, punctuation

Theodore Dreiser (1871–1945) novelist, journalist, *An American Tragedy*

Ralph Waldo Emerson (1803–82) New England philosopher, poet, essayist

William Faulkner (1897–1962) Nobel laureate, *Sanctuary*

F. Scott Fitzgerald (1896–1940) novelist, short stories, *The Great Gatsby*

Robert Frost (1894–1963) poet

Ernest Hemingway (1899–1961) Nobel laureate, *A Farewell to Arms*

O. Henry (1862–1910) short story writer

Washington Irving (1783–1859) essayist, historian, *The Legend of Sleepy Hollow*

Henry James (1843–1916) novelist, critic, *The Portrait of a Lady, The Turn of the Screw*

Sinclair Lewis (1885–1951) novelist, playwright, *Babbit*

Jack London (1876–1916) novelist, *The Call of the Wild*

Herman Melville (1819–91) novelist, *Moby Dick*

Eugene O'Neil (1888–1953) Nobel laureate, *Long Voyage Home, The Iceman Cometh*

Lincoln Steffens (1866–1936) muckraking author, *The Shame of Cities*

Gertrude Stein (1874–1916) poet, novelist, conducted famous literary salon

John Steinbeck (1902–68) Nobel laureate, *The Grapes of Wrath*

Harriet Beecher Stowe (1811–96) novelist, *Uncle Tom's Cabin*

James Thurber (1894–1961) humourist, cartoonist, *The Unicorn in the Garden*

Mark Twain (Samuel Clemens) (1835–1910) *Tom Sawyer, Huckleberry Finn*

John Updike (1932–) novelist, short story writer, *Rabbit Run*

Walt Whitman (1819–92) poet, *Leaves of Grass*

Tennessee Williams (1914–) playwright, *Streetcar Named Desire*

Frank Yerby (1916–) best-selling black author, *Foxes of Harrow*

Artists

Thomas Eakins (1844–1916) *The Chess Players*

Winslow Homer (1836–1910) painter of sea scenes, landscapes

Edward Hopper (1882–1967) realistic painter

Grandma Moses (1860–1916) primitive; took up painting at age of 78

Jackson Pollock (1912–56) abstractionist

Frederic Remington (1861–1900) painter of scenes of western America

James Whistler (1834–1903) painter; great success in Europe; *Whistler's Mother*

Architects

Buckminster Fuller (1895––) inventor; geodesic domes

Ludwig Mies van der Rohe (1886–1969) Seagram building (New York)

Eero Saarinen (1910–61) Gateway Arch (St. Louis), TWA Terminal (New York)

Frank Lloyd Wright (1869–1959) innovator

Musicians

Louis Armstrong (1900–71) jazz trumpeter and singer

Leonard Bernstein (1918–) *West Side Story*

Aaron Copeland (1900–) *Appalachian Spring*

Bob Dylan (1941–) poet, composer, singer

John Philip Sousa (1854–1932) band leader; composer of stirring marches

George Gershwin (1898–1937) *Porgy and Bess, Rhapsody in Blue*

Benny Goodman (1909–) jazz clarinetist

Elvis Presley (1935–) rock 'n roll singer

Beverly Sills (1929–) opera singer

W. P. Handy (1873–1958) blues composer

Scientists and inventors

Alexander Graham Bell (1847–1922) inventor of telephone; worked on flying machines

Luther Burbank (1849–1926) plant scientist; developed many new species

Thomas A. Edison (1847–1931) inventor of cinema, phonograph, light bulb, etc.

Albert Einstein (1879–1955) physicist, philosopher; theory of relativity

Henry Ford (1863–1947) automobile executive; first assembly line

Robert Fulton (1765–1815) first successful steamboat; many other inventions; painter

Robert Goddard (1882–1945) physicist, first liquid fuel rocket launch

Elias Howe (1819–67) invented sewing machine

Samuel Morse (1791–1872) portrait painter; perfecter of telegraph

J. Robert Oppenheimer (1904–67) scientist; "Father of the atomic bomb"

Linus Pauling (1901–) chemist, peace advocate; two Nobel prizes

Eli Whitney (1765–1825) inventor of cotton gin, concept of interchangeable parts

Norbert Wiener (1894–1964) early work on computers, cybernetics

The Wright Brothers: Orville (1871–1948) and Wilbur (1867–1912) inventors of first successful aeroplane

Reference
The Economy

Facts and figures

Total wealth produced (1972), 1,691 billion dollars.
Economic growth rate: 3.2% per year (1965-70)
Main sources of income:
Agriculture: grains, cotton, tobacco, nuts, fruit, sugar cane, cattle, sheep, hogs.
Mining: petroleum, metals (iron, copper, gold), coal, natural gas.
Manufacturing: machinery, motor vehicles, aircraft, food, tobacco, clothing, chemicals, furniture, timber, instruments.
Services: tourism, medical care, banking, real estate, radio and tele-vision, railroads, airlines, stocks, education.
Main trading partners: Canada, Japan, the Common Market, South America.
Currency: the dollar. $1 equals approximately £0·42 (42 pence).

What is imported and exported

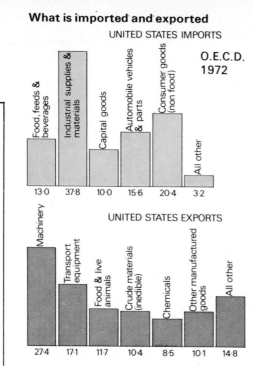

UNITED STATES IMPORTS

O.E.C.D. 1972

Food, feeds & beverages	Industrial supplies & materials	Capital goods	Automobile vehicles & parts	Consumer goods (non food)	All other
13·0	37·8	10·0	15·6	20·4	3·2

UNITED STATES EXPORTS

Machinery	Transport equipment	Food & live animals	Crude materials (inedible)	Chemicals	Other manufactured goods	All other
27·4	17·1	11·7	10·4	8·5	10·1	14·8

Heavy machinery is by far the most valuable export item for the U.S., followed by motor vehicles, food (mostly grain), and other manufactured goods. Petroleum, food (mostly meat and fish), electrical apparatus, and motor vehicles are among the leading American imports.

The fight against inflation

After many years of relative stability, the economic situation in the United States tended to become confused, erratic, and unpredictable in the mid 1970s. Following the great depression of the 1930s, and the wartime economic boom, wages and prices rose slowly and steadily through the 1950s and 1960s, with several recessions. But a combination of events, including the very expensive Vietnam War, without sufficient tax increases to pay for it, a worldwide series of crop failures in 1972, and the great petrol shortage following the Arab-Israeli war of 1973, tended to speed up inflation.

Wages and prices were frozen in August 1971, but following the end of most controls in January 1973, prices zoomed upwards. Food prices rose 20% in 1973 alone, and there was no end in sight. Inflation, and the effect of several devaluations of the dollar, has meant that a wage earner is able to buy less each year than the year before, despite rising salaries and wages.

Economists seemed quite uncertain what the middle and long range future held in store. World-wide competition for declining raw materials makes it seem unlikely that prices will come back down. But there remains much faith in "good old Yankee ingenuity and know-how", coupled with the feeling (as Sinclair Lewis wrote, sarcastically in a similar context), that "It can't happen here." Only time will tell.

Agriculture in the U.S.A.

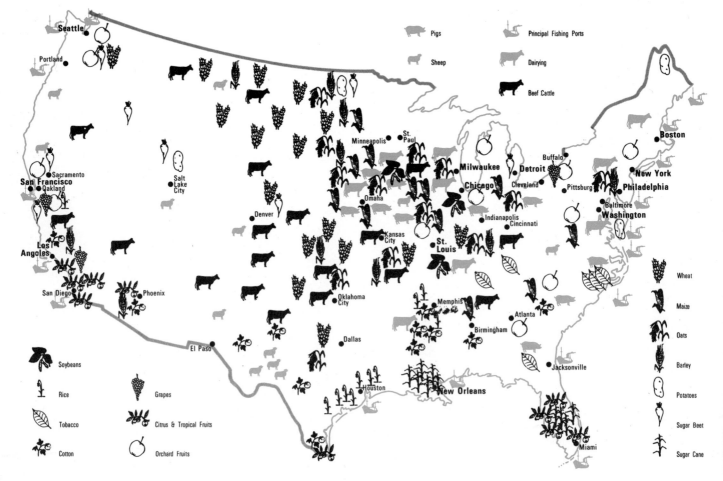

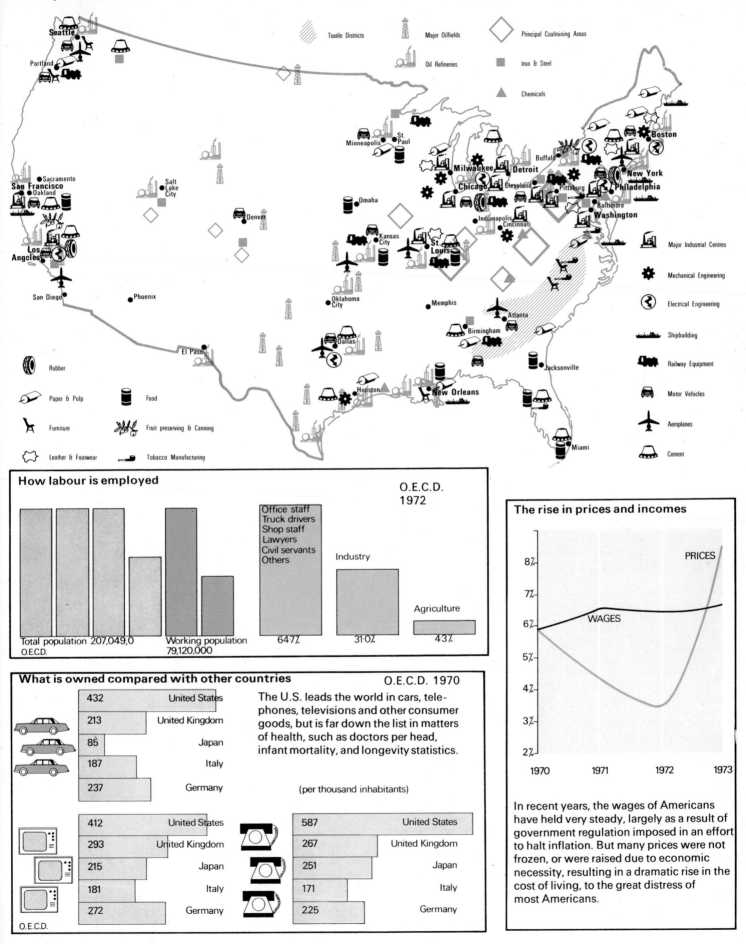

Industry in the U.S.A.

Legend:
- Textile Districts
- Major Oilfields
- Principal Coalmining Areas
- Oil Refineries
- Iron & Steel
- Chemicals
- Rubber
- Paper & Pulp
- Food
- Furniture
- Fruit preserving & Canning
- Leather & Footwear
- Tobacco Manufacturing
- Major Industrial Centres
- Mechanical Engineering
- Electrical Engineering
- Shipbuilding
- Railway Equipment
- Motor Vehicles
- Aeroplanes
- Cement

Cities labelled on map: Seattle, Portland, Sacramento, San Francisco, Oakland, Los Angeles, San Diego, Phoenix, Salt Lake City, Denver, El Paso, Dallas, Houston, Oklahoma City, Kansas City, Omaha, Minneapolis, St. Paul, Milwaukee, Chicago, St. Louis, Memphis, New Orleans, Birmingham, Atlanta, Jacksonville, Miami, Detroit, Cleveland, Cincinnati, Indianapolis, Buffalo, Pittsburg, Washington, Baltimore, Philadelphia, New York, Boston

How labour is employed
O.E.C.D. 1972

Total population 207,049,0
O.E.C.D.

Working population 79,120,000

- Office staff, Truck drivers, Shop staff, Lawyers, Civil servants, Others — 64.7%
- Industry — 31.0%
- Agriculture — 4.3%

What is owned compared with other countries
O.E.C.D. 1970

Cars:
432	United States
213	United Kingdom
85	Japan
187	Italy
237	Germany

(per thousand inhabitants)

Televisions:
412	United States
293	United Kingdom
215	Japan
181	Italy
272	Germany

Telephones:
587	United States
267	United Kingdom
251	Japan
171	Italy
225	Germany

O.E.C.D.

The U.S. leads the world in cars, telephones, televisions and other consumer goods, but is far down the list in matters of health, such as doctors per head, infant mortality, and longevity statistics.

The rise in prices and incomes

PRICES
WAGES

(Vertical axis: 2% to 8%; Horizontal axis: 1970, 1971, 1972, 1973)

In recent years, the wages of Americans have held very steady, largely as a result of government regulation imposed in an effort to halt inflation. But many prices were not frozen, or were raised due to economic necessity, resulting in a dramatic rise in the cost of living, to the great distress of most Americans.

Gazetteer

STATES AND TERRITORIES
The name is followed by the map location, the population, and the capital city.

Alabama (33N 87W) 3,444,165, Montgomery. "Heart of Dixie"; timber and cotton crops.

Alaska (65N 150W) 302,173, Juneau. Largest, coldest, least-populated state.

Arizona (34N 112W) 1,772,482, Phoenix. The Grand Canyon State; deserts, tourism.

Arkansas (35N 93W) 1,923,295, Little Rock. Hot springs, cotton, timber, rice, chickens.

California (35N 120W) 19,953,134, Sacramento. Biggest population; budget exceeds all but 5 foreign nations; leading agricultural producer; aerospace, oil, films, tourism.

Colorado (38N 114W) 2,207,259, Denver. Mountains, gold and silver mines, skiing.

Connecticut (42N 73W) 3,032,217, Hartford. Industrial cities, picturesque villages.

Delaware (39N 75W) 548,104, Dover. Huge chemical industry; farming, shellfish.

Florida (27N 82W) 6,789,443, Tallahassee. Winter resorts, leading citrus producer.

Georgia (32N 83W) 4,589,575, Atlanta. Peanuts, marble, farming, peaches, wood.

Hawaii (20N 115W) 769,913, Honolulu; semi-tropic islands; last state 1959.

Idaho (45N 115W) 713,008, Boise. Potatoes, silver, rugged canyons, hunting, fishing.

Illinois (40N 90W) 11,113,976, Springfield. Highly agricultural and industrial. Nuclear research; coal, corn, oil, meat processing.

Indiana (40N 87W) 5,193,669, Indianapolis. Steel plants, mobile homes, sand dunes.

Iowa (43N 94W) 2,825,041, Des Moines. Farms, farm industry, hogs, corn, soybeans.

Kansas (38N 98W) 2,249,071, Topeka. Wheat, light aircraft, helium, medical research.

Kentucky (38N 85W) 3,219,311, Frankfort. Tobacco, coal, race horses, Fort Knox gold.

Louisiana (32N 93W) 3,643,180, Baton Rouge. Sweet potatoes, sugar cane; jazz.

Maine (45N 70W) 993,663, Augusta. Lobsters, potatoes, rugged coast, dense forests.

Maryland (39N 76W) 3,922,399, Annapolis. Nearly divided by Chesapeake Bay; seafood.

Massachusetts (42N 72W) 5,689,170, Boston. Historic sites, famous schools, Harvard, M.I.T.; shipbuilding, manufacturing.

Michigan (43N 85W) 8,875,083, Lansing. Auto manufacture, fruit crops, iron ore. Divided in two parts by Lake Michigan.

Minnesota (45N 95W) 3,805,069, St. Paul. Iron ore, prairies, resorts, 15,000 lakes.

Mississippi (33N 90W) 2,216,912, Jackson. Deepest south; cotton, paper, pecans.

Missouri (38N 93W) 4,677,399, Jefferson City. Gateway to west; aerospace, lead, hogs.

Montana (48N 110W) 694,409, Helena. High mountains, vast plains, wheat, rye.

Nebraska (42N 100W) 1,483,791, Lincoln. Only one-house legislature; meat, grain.

Nevada (40N 118W) 488,738, Carson City. Legal gambling, resorts, desert, mountains.

New Hampshire (43N 72W) 737,681, Concord. Forests, lakes; maple sugar and syrup.

New Jersey (40N 74W) 7,168,164, Trenton. Densest population; shipping, farming.

New Mexico (35N 107W) 1,016,000, Santa Fe. Spanish culture; deserts, caves, mountains.

New York (43N 75W) 18,241,266, Albany. Leads in manufacturing (clothing, printing, paper, cameras, etc.) U.N. headquarters. Grapes, clover, apples, tourism.

North Carolina (36N 80W) 5,082,059, Raleigh. Textiles, furniture, bricks, tobacco.

North Dakota (48N 100W) 617,761, Bismarck. Prairies, scenic badlands, hunting.

Ohio (40N 83W) 10,652,017, Columbus. Heavy industry, tyres, coal, tools, glass. 14 major universities; football hall of fame.

Oklahoma (35N 97W) 2,559,253, Oklahoma City. Rolling plains; oil, wheat, cattle.

Oregon (44N 122W) 2,091,385, Salem. Vast forests, mountains, valleys; berries, pears.

Pennsylvania (42N 77W) 11,793,909, Harrisburg. Historic landmarks, steel production, coal, farming, sausages, ice cream, grapes.

Rhode Island (42N 72W) 949,723, Providence. Smallest state, highly industrial.

South Carolina (33N 81W) 2,590,516, Columbia. Tobacco, cotton; ports, beaches.

South Dakota (44N 100W) 666,257, Pierre. Rich farms, rye, oats; Black Hills, gold.

Tennessee (36N 87W) 3,924,164, Nashville. Bluegrass land; Smoky Mountains; chemicals.

Texas (33N 100W) 11,196,730, Austin. 2nd largest state; leads in oil, cattle, sheep, cotton. Formerly an independent republic.

Utah (40N 112W) 1,059,273, Salt Lake City. Founded by Mormons; manufacturing.

Vermont (44N 73W) 444,732, Montpelier. Stoneworking, quarries, forests, mountains.

Virginia (38N 77W) 4,648,494, Richmond. Colonial heritage; famous battlefields; tobacco, peanuts, lumber, furniture.

Washington (47N 120W) 3,409,169, Olympia. Aircraft manufacture, lumber, tourism.

Wisconsin (45N 90W) 4,417,933, Madison. America's dairyland; milk, cheese, farming.

Wyoming (43N 107W) 332,416, Cheyenne. The wild west; mountains, plains, mines.

District of Columbia (38N 77W) 756,510, Washington. Not a state; seat of Federal government: the White House, Capitol, Supreme Court. Limited self-government.

Puerto Rico (19N 77W) 2,712,033, San Juan. Commonwealth associated with U.S.; natives are U.S. citizens; Spanish-speaking island.

Virgin Islands (17N 63W) 62,468, Charlotte Amalie. Administered by U.S.; natives are U.S. citizens. Tourism, rum, watches.

LARGEST CITIES
Each city name is followed by its state, map location, and 1970 population.

New York, New York (40 45N 73 59W) 7,894,862; largest city.

Chicago, Illinois (41 52N 87 38W) 3,369,359. Midwest port; meat, steel, heavy industry.

Los Angeles, California (34 03N 118 14W) 2,809,596; films, aerospace, resorts.

Philadelphia, Pennsylvania (39 56N 75 09W) 1,950,098. Birthplace of the nation.

Detroit, Michigan (42 19N 83 02W) 1,513,601. Motor City, on Canadian border.

Houston, Texas (29 45N 95 21W) 1,232,802. Fastest-growing major city; gulf port.

Baltimore, Maryland (39 17N 76 36W) 905,759. Port, 25 colleges and universities.

Dallas, Texas (32 47N 96 47W) 844,401. Financial centre of southwest.

Washington, D.C. (38 53N 77 00W) 756,510. Nation's capital; over 70% black.

Cleveland, Ohio (41 29N 81 41W) 750,879. Industrial city on shores of Lake Erie.

Indianapolis, Indiana (39 46N 86 09W) 744,743. Industrial centre.

Milwaukee, Wisconsin (43 02N 87 54W) 717,372. German heritage.

San Francisco, California (37 46N 122 24W) 715,674. Most popular city.

San Diego, California (32 42N 117 09W) 697,027. Near Mexico; port, naval centre.

San Antonio, Texas (29 25N 98 29W) 654,153. Mexican heritage.

Boston, Massachusetts (42 21N 71 03W) 641,071. Founded by Puritans; cultural centre.

Memphis, Tennessee (35 08N 90 03W) 623,530. World's largest hardwood, cotton.

St. Louis, Missouri (38 37N 90 12W) 622,236. The gateway to the west.

New Orleans, Louisiana (29 56N 90 04W) 593,471. Home of jazz; French heritage.

NATURAL AND SCENIC FEATURES

Appalachian Mountains, stretching from Alabama to Pennsylvania.

Columbia River (46N 120W) 1,214 miles long.

Death Valley (37N 117W) Lowest spot in western hemisphere; 282 feet below sea level.

Everglades (27N 81W) Great primeval swamp land of central Florida.

Great Salt Lake (42N 113W) 25% salt density.

Lake Erie (42N 82W) 9,910 sq. miles.

Lake Huron (45N 83W) 23,100 sq. miles.

Lake Michigan (43N 87W) 22,300 sq. miles; only Great Lake entirely inside U.S.

Lake Ontario (43N 78W) 7,550 sq. miles.

Lake Superior (48N 87W) 31,700 sq. miles; largest of the five Great Lakes.

Mauna Loa (19N 156W) 13,680 ft., active volcano in Hawaiian Islands.

Mississippi River (35N 90W) "Ol' man river"; divides America, 2,350 miles long.

Missouri River (40N 95W) 2,533 miles long; longest in U.S.; flows into Mississippi.

Mojave Desert (35N 115W) thousands of square miles of California, Nevada, Arizona.

Mt. McKinley (54N 150W) 20,320 ft., highest peak in North America; in Alaska.

Mt. Whitney (37N 118W) 14,494 ft., highest U.S. peak outside Alaska; near Death Valley.

Niagara Falls (43N 79W) Spectacular waterfalls right on U.S.-Canadian border.

Ohio River (38N 85W) 1,306 miles long.

Painted Desert (37N 110W) multi-coloured sands, petrified wood, in Arizona.

Rocky Mountains, peaks up to 14,000 feet, stretching from Canada to Mexico.

Snake River (45N 117W) 1,038 miles long.

Yellowstone Park (45N 110W) world's first national park, founded in 1872.

Index

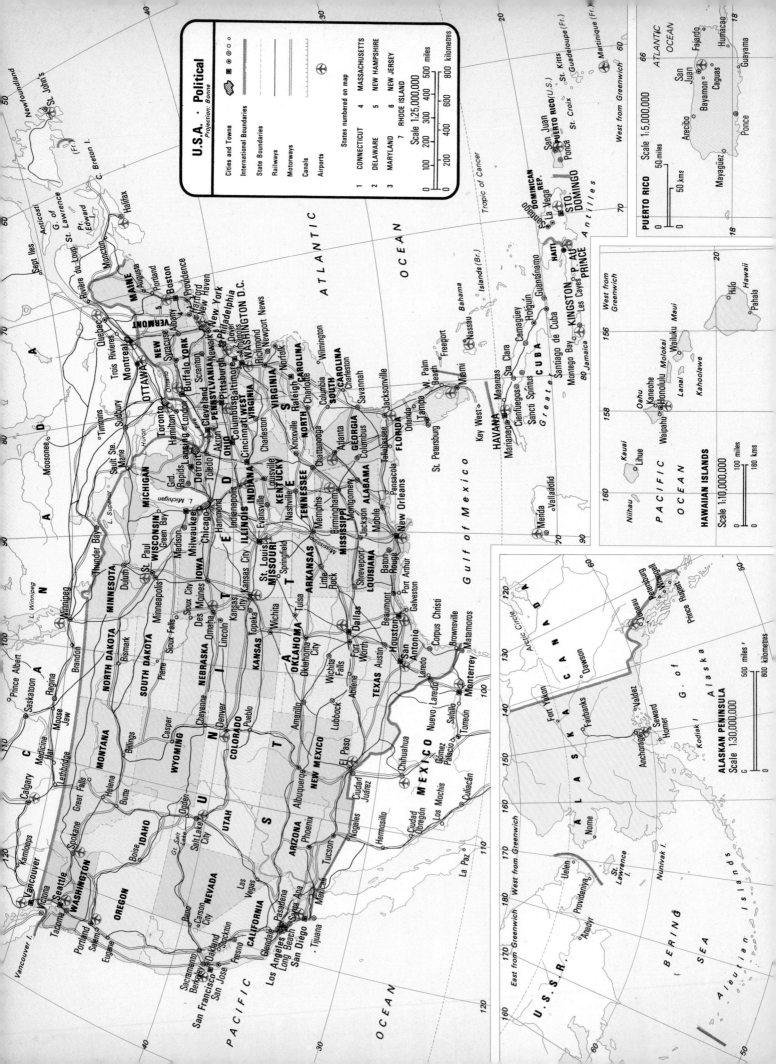

U.S.A. · Political
Projection: Bonne

Cities and Towns
International Boundaries
State Boundaries
Railways
Motorways
Canals
Airports

States numbered on map

1	CONNECTICUT	4	MASSACHUSETTS
2	DELAWARE	5	NEW HAMPSHIRE
3	MARYLAND	6	NEW JERSEY
		7	RHODE ISLAND

Scale 1:25,000,000

0 100 200 300 400 500 miles
0 200 400 600 800 kilometres

PUERTO RICO   Scale 1:5,000,000
50 miles
50 kms

HAWAIIAN ISLANDS
Scale 1:10,000,000
100 miles
160 kms

ALASKAN PENINSULA
Scale 1:30,000,000
500 miles
800 kilometres